iMac, iBook, and G3 Troubleshooting Pocket Reference

S0-BND-628

Don Rittner

McGraw-Hill

New York   San Francisco   Washington, D.C.   Auckland   Bogotá
Caracas   Lisbon   London   Madrid   Mexico City   Milan
Montreal   New Delhi   San Juan   Singapore
Sydney   Tokyo   Toronto

McGraw-Hill

*A Division of The **McGraw·Hill** Companies*

1 2 3 4 5 6 7 8 9 0   AGM/AGM   0 5 4 3 2 1 0

ISBN 0-07-212468-7

The sponsoring editor for this book was Michael Sprague and the production manager was Claire Stanley. This book was set in Century Schoolbook by Patricia Wallenburg.

Printed and bound by Quebecor / Martinsburg.

For Nancy, Christopher, Kevin, Jack, Jason, and Jennifer

Acknowledgments

Many Macintosh people selfishly share their talent and spend hours of time giving out advice, and sharing their experiences, so others avoid the pitfalls of computing. Many people have shared their knowledge and helped me in the preparation of this book. I thank the following people for their contributions:

Apple Computer, Aron Suzuk, Andrew Welch, Bill Kane, Brenda Tupper, Brian Breslin, Brock Kyle, Cabel Sasser, Chris Kidwell, Chris Silverberg, Darren Sea, Darren Seay, David Tiberio, Erik J. Barzeski, Eric Dahlinger, Eric Prentice, Gareth Anderson, Gideon Greenspan, Greg Nye, J. Zack, Jason Pierce, Jayme Curtis, Jeff, Keller, Jeff Mangels, Jeremiah L. Glodoveza, Joe Ryan, John A. Vink, John Allsopp, John C. Mozena, John Stiles, Joseph C. Lee, Joseph M. Saul, Kelly Crowe, Laini Nance, Lucas Roebuck, Matthew M. Linton, Michael Yee, Mike Fahrion, Mike Kubovcik, Peter Li, Phil Shapiro, Rolf Braun, Ron Lichty, Scott J. Kleper, Scott William, Sean Mcbride, Shawn King, Stephanie Da Silva, Steve Chamberlin, Sue Nail, Thorsten Lemke, and to those I inadvertently left out, my apologies.

Special thanks go to Nancy, Christopher, Kevin, and Jack.

I especially thank Ken Ackley, an Apple-certified technician, for his expertise in putting together Chapters 3 and 4 and for photographing the upgrade paths in Chapter 3, and to Jason and Jen for lending a hand or two.

Special thanks to Michael Sprague and Sharon A. Linsenbach from McGraw-Hill, and to Patty Wallenburg for making it all look good! Finally, thanks to Margot Maley from Waterside.

Contents

Introduction

This book is for you if you recently purchased an Apple Macintosh G3 computer, or have been using one for some time. This is a nontechnical troubleshooting and repair book for the average Mac user. It is not designed for the techie and you don't have to be one to make sure your G3 is well tuned and free of trouble. Moreover, armed with this book, a screwdriver, and a little confidence, you can save yourself some time and money fixing, all by yourself, those small problems that creep up once a while. Apple has ensured that only the best parts go into making a Macintosh computer, but even the best computer in the world can have problems sometime.

This book is designed to show you how to troubleshoot common problems and take the basic precautions using the best maintenance tips. It also shows you how to troubleshoot problems when you have them, upgrade your Mac hardware and software, and when to take your Mac to a certified Apple technician if all else fails. Most of the time you can fix and upgrade your G3 by yourself.

There are several common problems that all Macs have experienced. Chapter One describes how you can avoid those common problems by taking a few precautions like rebuilding your Mac's desktop, optimizing your hard drive, checking for viruses daily, backing up your data regularly, replacing corrupted preference files, and ensuring that you have the latest drivers and operating system software to keep your Mac well tuned.

Chapter 2 builds on Chapter 1 by going into more detail about why certain common problems occur on the Mac: software conflicts, monitor freezes and computer hangups, hard drive defragmentation, and more. Once you understand the underlying functions of the system software and how the Mac interacts with it, you can avoid these kinds of risks by making preventative tips a regular chore.

Chapter 3 contains several step-by-step upgrade paths for various G3 models. Here you can learn how to easily upgrade your computer memory, add video RAM, an extra SCSI hard drive, or PCI card, with complete step-by-step instructions and illustrations to guide you along the way.

Chapter 4 is a step by step troubleshooting guide on all models of the G3 from the desktop G3 to the iBook. This chapter gives the possible reasons why you are having troubles with your system software, video, peripherals, printers, networking, and more. Several possible fixes are offered, including Apple's recommendations, before you are encouraged to bring the Mac to a certified Apple technician for repair.

Chapter 5 is your online guide for getting the latest information, help, software updates, news, prices on new and used equipment, and peripherals, and the latest offerings and updates from the Internet. There are thousands of fellow Mac users online who provide free technical help, review the latest software and hardware products, provide tutorials and articles, even repair tips, and carry on daily conversations in mailing lists, bulletin boards, chat rooms, and Usenet newsgroups. This chapter shows you where to find all of this on the Net.

Chapter 6 discusses several life-saving disk recovery programs on the market that can help you diagnose and fix software problems. The programs are inexpensive but power packed, with a variety of tools to troubleshoot and fix almost any problem that can occur on your G3. Several of these programs actually monitor your computer's behavior and will alert you to problems before they happen.

Most G3 models are upgradable to new and faster processors. Chapter 7 shows you where to obtain your processor upgrades or memory modules, and other hardware upgrades and how to find the best prices for both new and used equipment. You will find that it is possible to upgrade most G3 models, and even some earlier PowerMac non-G3 models, for many years to come.

How to Use This Book

First, read Chapters 1, 2, and 6 to familiarize yourself with the basic maintenance and preventative issues relating to your Mac. Read Chapter Five next so you can learn how to keep abreast of the latest news, updates, and issues regarding the Mac from the Internet. If you have a problem with your Mac then read Chapter Four to isolate the problem and see if you can fix it yourself. Finally if you are looking to upgrade your Mac's memory, hardware, or processor, read Chapters Three and Seven.

Finally, I encourage you to purchase an Apple warranty for your Mac. When you reach those rare moments when there is a real hardware failure that you cannot fix, you can have peace of mind knowing you can bring the Mac to a certified Apple technician. Apple warranties are not expensive. Learn more about them from the Apple Web site (**www.apple.com**).

G3 Models Released

Since the introduction of the first G3 Mac in November 1997, Apple has released 35 models in the form of desktops, minitowers, towers, laptops, servers, and the innovative iMac and iBook models. All the models use the PowerPC 750 G3 microprocessor running at various speeds, as shown below. This book can be used for all models.

G3 model name

Desktops and towers

- **Power Macintosh G3/233MHz Desktop**—This model came with 32 MB of RAM, a 4.0 GB hard drive, and ATI 3D Rage II+ (Rage Pro after May 1, 1998) graphics acceleration. It was introduced on November 10, 1997 and discontinued on August 12, 1998.

- **Power Macintosh G3/233 MHz MiniTower**—This model came with 32 MB of RAM, a 4.0 GB hard drive, an internal Zip drive, and ATI 3D Rage II+ (Rage Pro after May 1, 1998) graphics acceleration. It was introduced on November 10, 1997 and discontinued on July 7, 1998.

- **Power Macintosh G3/266 MHz Desktop**—This model came with 32 MB of RAM, a 4.0 GB hard drive, built-in Zip drive, and ATI 3D Rage II+ (Rage Pro after May 1, 1998, Rage Pro Turbo after August 12, 1998) graphics acceleration. It was introduced on November 10, 1997 and discontinued on December 14, 1998 .

- **Power Macintosh G3/266 MHz MiniTower**—This model came with 32 MB of RAM, a 6.0 GB hard drive, an internal Zip drive, and ATI 3D Rage II+ (Rage Pro after May 1, 1998) graphics acceleration. It was introduced on November 10, 1997 and discontinued on August 12, 1998.

- **Power Macintosh G3/300 MHz Desktop**—This model cam with 32 MB of RAM, a 6.0 GB hard drive, built-in Zip drive, and ATI 3D Rage II+ (Rage

Pro after May 1, 1998, Rage Pro Turbo after August 12, 1998) graphics acceleration. It was introduced on March 17, 1998 and discontinued on December 14, 1998.

- **Power Macintosh G3/300 MHz MiniTower**— This model came with 64 MB of RAM, a 4.0 or 8.0 GB hard drive, an internal Zip drive, and ATI 3D Rage II+ (Rage Pro after May 1, 1998, Rage Pro Turbo after August 12, 1998) graphics acceleration. It was introduced on March 17, 1998 and discontinued on December 14, 1998.

- **Power Macintosh G3/333 MHz MiniTower**— This model came with 128 MB of RAM, a 9.0 GB hard drive, an internal Zip drive, ATI 3D Rage Pro Turbo graphics acceleration, and a DVD Video and A/V personality card . It was introduced on August 12, 1998 (didn't ship until October 1, 1998) and discontinued on December 14, 1998.

Blue & whites

- **Power Macintosh G3/300 MHz (Blue & White)**—This model came with 64 MB of RAM, a 6.0 GB hard drive, and an ATI 3D Rage 128 GL video card with 16 MB of VRAM. It was introduced on January 5, 1999 and discontinued on June 1, 1999.

- **Power Macintosh G3/350 MHz (Blue & White)**—This model came with 64 MB or 128 MB of RAM, a 6.0 GB or 12.0 GB hard drive, a Zip drive (optional), and an ATI 3D Rage 128 GL video card with 16 MB of VRAM. It was introduced on January 5, 1999 and discontinued on August 31, 1999.

- **Power Macintosh G3/400 MHz (Blue & White)**—This model came with 64 MB or 128 MB of RAM, a 9.0 or 12.0 GB Ultra2 SCSI hard drive, and an ATI 3D Rage 128 GL video card with 16 MB of VRAM. It was introduced on January 5, 1999 and discontinued on August 31, 1999.

- **Power Macintosh G3/450 MHz (Blue & White)**—This model came with 128 MB of RAM, a 9.0 GB Ultra2 SCSI hard drive, and an ATI 3D Rage 128 GL video card with 16 MB of VRAM. It was introduced on June 1, 1999 and discontinued on August 31, 1999.

Servers

- **Macintosh Server G3/233 MHz MiniTower**—This model came with 64 MB of RAM, a 4.0 GB hard drive, and a preinstalled bundle of Apple server software. It was introduced on March 2, 1998 and discontinued on September 1, 1998.

- **Macintosh Server G3/266 MHz MiniTower**—This model came with 128 MB of RAM, a 4.0 GB hard drive, and a preinstalled bundle of Apple server software. It was introduced on March 2, 1998 and discontinued on September 1, 1998.

- **Macintosh Server G3/300 MHz MiniTower**—This model came with 64 MB or 128 MB of RAM, a 4.0 GB hard drive, and a preinstalled bundle of Apple server software. It was introduced on March 17, 1998 and discontinued on December 14, 1998.

- **Macintosh Server G3/333 MHz MiniTower**—This model came with 128 MB of RAM, dual 9.0 GB hard drives, and a preinstalled bundle of Apple server software. It was introduced on September 1, 1998 and discontinued on December 14, 1998.

- **Macintosh Server G3/350 MHz (Blue & White)**—This model came with 128 MB of RAM, a 9.0 GB Ultra2 SCSI hard drive, an ATI 3D Rage 128 GL video card with 16 MB of VRAM, and the preinstalled "AppleShare Solution Kit." It was introduced on January 5, 1999 and discontinued on June 1, 1999.

- **Macintosh Server G3/400 MHz (Blue & White)**—This model came with 128 MB or 256 MB of RAM, one, two, or three 9.0 GB Ultra2 SCSI hard drives, an ATI 3D Rage 128 GL video card with 16 MB of VRAM, and the preinstalled "AppleShare Solution Kit." It was introduced on January 5, 1999 and discontinued on August 31, 1999.

- **Macintosh Server G3/450 MHz (Blue & White)**—This model came with 256 MB of RAM, two 9.0 GB Ultra2 SCSI hard drives, an ATI 3D Rage 128 GL video card with 16 MB of VRAM, and the preinstalled "AppleShare Solution Kit" or MacOS X Server. It was introduced on June 1, 1999 and discontinued on August 31, 1999.

Powerbook

- **Macintosh PowerBook G3 MHz (Orig)**—This model came with 32 MB of RAM, and a 5.0 GB hard drive in a black portable case with a 12.1" color active-matrix display, hot-swappable bays, four-speaker system, and zoomed video support. It was introduced on November 10, 1997 and discontinued on March 14, 1998.

- **Macintosh PowerBook G3/233 MHz (WallStreet)**—This model came with 32 MB of RAM, a 2.0 GB hard drive with either a 12.1" STN, 13.3" TFT, or 14.1" TFT color display (3.), dual hot-swappable bays, stereo speaker system, 2D/3D graphics acceleration, an "fn" key which created a numerical keyboard, S-video output, and zoomed video support. It was introduced on May 6, 1998 and discontinued on May 10, 1999.

- **Macintosh PowerBook G3/250 MHz**—This model came with 32 MB of RAM, a 2.0 GB or 4.0 GB hard drive, with either a 12.1" STN, 13.3" TFT, or 14.1" TFT color display, dual hot-swappable bays, stereo speaker system, 2D/3D graphics acceleration, an "fn" key which created a numerical keyboard, S-video output, and zoomed video support. Introduced on May 6, 1998 and discontinued on September 1, 1998.

- **Macintosh PowerBook G3/266 MHz**—This model came with 64 MB of RAM, and a 4.0 GB hard drive with a 14.1" TFT color display, dual hot-swappable bays, stereo speaker system, 2D/3D graphics acceleration, an "fn" key which created a numerical keyboard, S-video output, and zoomed video support. It was introduced on September 1, 1998 and discontinued on May 10, 1999.

- **Macintosh PowerBook G3/292 MHz**—This model came with 64 MB of RAM, and a 4.0 GB or 8.0 GB hard drive with a 13.3" or 14.1" TFT color display, dual hot-swappable bays, stereo speaker system, 2D/3D graphics acceleration, an "fn" key which created a numerical keyboard, S-video output, and zoomed video support. It was introduced on May 6, 1998 and discontinued on September 1, 1998.

- **Macintosh PowerBook G3/300 MHz**—This model came with 64 MB of RAM, and a 8.0 GB hard drive with a 14.1" TFT color display, dual hot-swappable bays, stereo speaker system, 2D/3D graphics acceleration, an "fn" key which created a numerical keyboard, S-video output, and zoomed video support. It was introduced on September 1, 1998 and discontinued on May 10, 1999.

- **Macintosh PowerBook G3/333 MHz (Bronze)**—This model comes with 64 MB of RAM, a 4.0 GB hard drive, and an ATI Rage LT Pro video controller with a 14.1" TFT color display. It was introduced on May 10, 1999 and is still being shipped.

- **Macintosh PowerBook G3/400 MHz (Bronze)**—This model comes with 64 MB of RAM, a 4.0 GB hard drive, and an ATI Rage LT Pro video controller with a 14.1" TFT color display. It was introduced on May 10, 1999 and is still being shipped.

All-in-one

- **G3 All-In-One G3/233 MHz**—This model came with 32 MB of RAM, a 4.0 GB hard drive, and ATI 3D Rage II+ (Rage Pro after May 1, 1998) graphics acceleration. Made available to North American education customers only. It was introduced on March 31, 1998 and discontinued on September 1, 1998.

- **G3 All-In-One G3/266 MHz**—This model came with 32 MB of RAM, a 4.0 GB hard drive, ATI 3D Rage II+ (Rage Pro after May 1, 1998) graphics acceleration. Made available to North American education customers only. It was introduced on March 31, 1998 and discontinued on October 17, 1998.

iMac

- **iMac (Rev. A & B) (233 MHZ)**—The Apple iMac (Rev. A & B) came with 32 MB of RAM, a 4.0 GB hard drive, and ATI Rage IIc (Rage Pro Turbo after October 26, 1998) graphics acceleration, USB, and a 15" color screen. It was introduced on May 6, 1998, although it didn't ship until August 15, 1999, and discontinued on January 5, 1999.

- **iMac (266 MHz)**—This model came with 32 MB of RAM, a 6.0 GB hard drive, and ATI Rage Pro Turbo graphics acceleration, USB, a 15" color screen, and was available in five colors: lime, strawberry, blueberry, grape, and tangerine. It was introduced on January 5, 1999 and discontinued on April 14, 1999.

- **iMac (333 MHz)**—This model came with 32 MB of RAM, a 6.0 GB hard drive, and ATI Rage Pro Turbo graphics acceleration with a 15" color screen and was available in five colors: lime, strawberry, blueberry, grape, and tangerine. It was introduced on April 14, 1999 and discontinued on October 5, 1999.

- **iMac (350 MHz)**—This model comes with 64 MB of RAM, a 6.0 GB hard drive, a slot-loading CD-ROM drive, ATI Rage 128 VR 2D/3D (2x AGP) graphics acceleration, a Harmon/Kardon designed sound system, and a 15" color screen. It was introduced on October 5, 1999 and is still being shipped.

- **iMac "DV" (400 MHz)**—This model comes with 64 MB of RAM, a 10.0 GB hard drive, a slot-loaded 4X DVD-ROM drive, ATI Rage 128 VR 2D/3D graphics acceleration, a Harman/Kardon designed sound system, a 15" color screen, and a choice of five colors, and includes FireWire and video-out ports. It was introduced on October 5, 1999 and is still being shipped.

- **iMac SE "DV" (400 MHz)**—This model available in translucent "graphite" comes with 128 MB of RAM, a 13.0 GB hard drive, a slot-loaded 4X DVD-ROM drive, ATI Rage 128 VR 2D/3D graphics acceleration, Harman/Kardon designed sound system, a 15" color screen, FireWire and video-out ports. It was introduced on October 5, 1999 and is still being shipped.

iBook

- **iBook (300 MHz)**—This model comes with 32 MB of RAM, a 3.2 GB hard drive, ATI Rage Mobility graphics acceleration, a 12.1" TFT active-matrix display, and "AirPort" wireless networking. It was introduced on July 21, 1999 and is still being shipped.

1

An Ounce of Prevention Is Worth a Pound of...

There are several routine maintenance tips that you should employ regularly to help avoid serious problems on your Mac. This is no different from tuning up your car periodically, or cleaning the house at least once a week. If you get into the habit of following the steps outlined below, chances are you will rarely have a problem with your Mac.

The tasks are:

- Back up your important documents daily
- Rebuild the desktop monthly
- Zap your parameter RAM quarterly
- Ventilate your Mac
- Check for viruses daily
- Run Disk First Aid or Norton Utilities
- Update drivers when needed
- Clean your Mac
- Defrag your hard drive when needed.

We will go into more detail on each one.

Back Up Your Files!

Back up your important files every day! There's no reason to lose important information.

You don't have to back up the actual software application programs (MS Office, Clarisworks, Quicken, etc.). Any programs you purchased or received with the computer can be reinstalled from their original masters. However, the files you create are priceless and if you lose them without having a backup copy you will kick yourself.

Many people recommend a backup process called the *grandfather approach*. You use two backup disks. The first disk is called the father and the second is the grandfather. Every day when you back up your files, you switch disks, so that there are two days' worth of backups. The grandfather disk becomes the father the next day, the father disk becomes the grandfather, and so on.

It is strongly suggested that you keep a backup at a different location. Keep one at your workplace, and take one with you or place one at a different location. When I am working on something really important I upload a copy to one of my e-mail addresses as a third option. Better be safe than sorry.

I prefer using Zip disks as my backup disks. There are streaming tape backup drives, optical disks, and even CD-ROM burners that are used for backup and archiving. Use whatever medium you feel comfortable with or can afford.

There are two ways you can back up your files. Use the drag and drop method. Grab the files you want to back up and drag them over to the Zip disk or use a commercial backup software. There are several to choose from.

Never store your backup disks or any disks on top of your computer, on a TV, or near any electrical device. The magnetic effects can scramble the information on your disks. Store your backups in an area where the temperature does not fluctuate a lot, preferably at room temperature.

Rebuild Your Desktop

Rebuilding your desktop does not require any tools but prevents certain problems from occurring such as your files losing their icons (they have a generic look), or not recognizing their parent application, which prevents the document from starting up when you double click on it.

Rebuilding the Desktop file, which is invisible, helps your Mac keep track of files stored on your hard drive more efficiently.

It does not take much to rebuild the desktop. Hold down the Apple (cloverleaf) key and Option key at the same time and start up your Mac. A dialog box will pop up and ask you if you are sure you want to perform the operation. Press OK. It will take a few minutes if you have a lot of files and you will see a status bar run across the screen. If the original desktop file is corrupted however, this may not be totally effective. Another small problem that occurs when you rebuild your desktop is the loss of all your comments in the Get Info box in your files or folders.

You can avoid both problems by using a free utility called TechTool (Figure 1.1) which allows you to rebuild the desktop by pushing one button, it also has the option of saving the Get Info comments and then replacing them after you do the rebuild. TechTool actually deletes the desktop file and creates a new one. You can obtain TechTool free by downloading it from the MicroMat Web site (**www.micromat.com**).

Rebuild your desktop at least once a month.

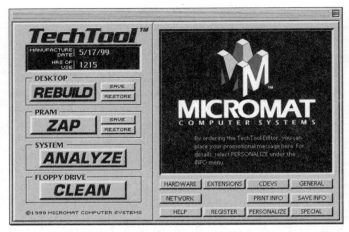

Figure 1.1   TechTool, a free utility from MicroMat lets you rebuild the desktop and other maintenance.

Reset Your Parameter RAM (Zapping the PRAM)

Parameter Random Access Memory (PRAM) is a small amount of memory in your Mac that is always on, and is continually powered by a small battery in your Mac. PRAM maintains certain preferences that you set, such as clock settings (alarm setting), printer port configuration and connection, monitor colors, speaker volume, double-click time, caret-blink time, menu blink, preferred system start-up disk, virtual memory, RAM disk, disk cache, and network settings, to name a few. These values are loaded into memory when you start your Mac. However, PRAM can and will get corrupted once in a while. The effects of this corruption range from crashing your computer to making it behave in a weird fashion.

To prevent this from occurring, or if you suspect that your PRAM needs resetting, you can reset, or zap, the PRAM. However, zapping the PRAM resets the Mac to the factory default settings for most of Apple's control panels like the General Controls,

Keyboard, Startup Disk, Mouse, and Map. You will need to go back and reset them to your preference.

To zap the PRAM, choose restart, or when you boot up your Mac hold the Command-Option-P-R keys and wait till you hear the startup tone. Keep holding the keys until you hear the tone for the second time, then let up. Go back to your Control Panels and reset them. I zap the PRAM once every 6 months.

You can use MicroMat's TechTool to zap the PRAM as well. MicroMat alerts you to a few possible side effects from zapping PRAM.

On certain inexpensive Apple color monitors and VGA monitors zapping may change to them to a green tint. This is due to a bug in some Mac PRAMs. If this happens to you, download the Apple Basic Color Monitor extension available from Apple's Web site (**www.apple.com**) or most online services. Some Macs may revert to 1-bit B&W, the factory default setting.

Another PRAM bug refuses to show color desktop patterns after zapping the PRAM. Open the Monitors control panel, select Black & White and then reselect your color setting. That should bring it back.

Be sure to disable any virus detection program you have before you zap.

Other potential problems, which can be corrected, according to MicroMat, include the StartUp Device's reverting to SCSI ID 0, or the factory default setting. The printer port will revert to AppleTalk Active, the factory default setting. The mouse speed will revert to the slow Tablet setting, the factory default setting.

A great benefit of using TechTool is saving your PRAM settings to disk. In the remote case that you have problems with your system after zapping the PRAM, TechTool will restore the previous settings.

Ventilate Your Mac

Do not place your Mac in an enclosed space where air cannot circulate as this can build up heat and damage your computer. A company called Vu-Ryte has an inexpensive stackable Mac stand that allows you to raise the Mac to any height by adding or deleting stands. Even with one, it allows air to circulate under and around the computer.

On certain models a thermal protection circuit will shut down the computer if it overheats and you will need to wait at least half an hour before restarting

Virus Checkers

Unfortunately, there are people who find it a thrill interfering with other people's computers and data. These malcontents create software programs that can damage or erase your hard drive, delete files, or replicate themselves faster than a budding yeast cell. These programs, known as Trojan Horses, worms, or viruses, will give you hours of grief if you catch one.

Fortunately for the Mac community, there are not a lot of these running around. There have been 20 or so that have appeared since the Mac was introduced, but only one or two are malicious enough to do serious damage.

Over the years, several free, shareware, and commercial virus detectors have been on the market that do a fine job of keeping your Mac free of these problems. Commercial virus killers like Norton AntiVirus, or Virex (**http://antivirus.miningco.com/**) also can do the job nicely. As new bugs enter the community, these commercial and shareware companies release patches or updaters to their software to kill them. Symantec, maker of Norton AntiVirus, has an automatic updater that will go onto its Web site, and grab the updater for you.

Mac viruses fall into four categories: autostart worms, system attackers, macro viruses, and hypercard viruses. They all behave a bit differently, but the result is the same, to foul up your data or hardware, or to harass you and make your life miserable for a while.

Get on the Net and go to MacVirus (**http://www.macvirus.com/**), a one-stop Web site that gives you the most information about every Mac virus. Here you can also download free and shareware virus killers, updaters from the commercial products; you can also read reviews of the various virus killer software products.

Never accept files from strangers, co-workers, or the Net without checking for a virus. Even the commercial online services like AOL check for viruses before they are made available for downloading. Get a virus checker. It is better to be safe than sorry.

Never download programs from the Net directly to your hard drive. I have a Zip disk that acts as a receiver of any downloads. After I download the programs to the Zip disk, I run AntiVirus and other checkers on the Zip disk and check for viruses. So far, I have never had a virus. I've been lucky.

DOS or Windows viruses don't affect Macs, but they can affect that part of a Mac using Virtual PC or SoftWindows, two Windows emulators. You may want to install DOS or Windows virus protection on these partitions as they are not protected by Macintosh virus detection programs.

Watch out for virus hoaxes. If you get an e-mail about the "Good Times" e-mail virus, forget it; it is an urban legend that appears at least once a year. In fact, the hoax becomes a virus, sort of. New Net folks start sending the virus report to all their friends, who then send it to all their friends, spreading it like a virus!

The Computer Incident Advisory Committee's (CIAC) Web site (**http://ciac.llnl.gov/ciac/CIACHoaxes.html**) is a good site to visit to keep yourself informed about real and fake viruses.

There are macro viruses that attack Microsoft Word files for Windows and Macintosh, but they can be detected and killed as well.

"Autostart worms" can be killed with Worm Guard (**http://hyperarchive.lcs.mit.edu/cgi-bin/**

NewSearch?key=WormGuard), or WormScanner
(**http://www.jwwalker.com/pages/worm. html**).
There are other worm killers. Be sure to check with
Mac Virus (**http://www.macvirus.com/**), one of the
best Mac virus Web sites.

Remember to check regularly for viruses

Subscribe to the Mac Virus mailing list so you can be
kept informed of new viruses that appear. To subscribe, send e-mail to:
listproc@listproc.bgsu.edu
In the body of the message, type:
subscribe mac-virus-announce YOUR FULL NAME

Defrag Your Hard Drive

A fragmented hard drive reminds me of my two-year-old
son. Fifteen minutes after I dress him in the morning, I
find a shoe in one room, shirt in the kitchen, diaper in
the foyer, the other shoe in the dining room, and so on.

Your Mac's hard drive is spinning around and as it
saves information it puts various chunks of a file on different parts of the spinning hard drive. After a while, if
you have tons of files, they could be scattered all over
the drive and it takes longer and longer for your hard
drive to put them together when you need to call them
up. This is called fragmentation. It slows things down.

Defragging or optimizing means to go and grab
those disparate files and piece them back together,
placing them closer together on the hard drive. This
increases your access time and your hard drive doesn't
work as hard.

Norton Utilities has an excellent defragger. It allows
you to optimize your disk for a variety of development
conditions from multimedia, software or CD-ROM development, or general use. It shows you visually how your
hard drive is fragmented before and after defragging.

I like to defrag at least once a month but you can wait a bit longer if you want. If you are using Norton Utilities FileSaver, it will tell you when defragging is needed.

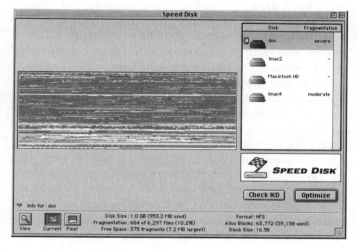

Figure 1.2 Hard drive before defragging.

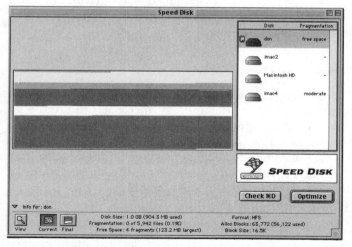

Figure 1.3 Hard drive after defragging.

Updating Drivers

Drivers are those software programs that let your Mac communicate with other hardware that is attached to it. You can have drivers for printers, scanners, hard drives, drawing pads, and the like. When you install a new version of the system software you also update the drivers to your hard drive. You should always make sure you are using the latest drivers for your products. This will avoid conflicts.

Before you install a new Apple system, check to see if all your peripheral drivers are compatible with the new system version. If not, you may want to wait until they are updated before you install the new system. This is especially important if you are not using Apple drivers on your hard drive. I like to visit the Web sites of those peripheral companies and download updated drivers before I update the system software.

As a rule, you should use the same formatting program to update the drivers as you used to format the disk originally. Be sure to back up your hard drive before you update the drivers or install new system software.

To keep track of all versions of software and drivers, visit the Web site Version Tracker at **http://www. versiontracker.com/**.

Clean Your Mac

This may seem like a minor thing, but dust gets into the guts of your Mac and can increase the fatigue on electrical components. Use a soft linen towel with warm water to clean the monitor to avoid eye fatigue. Never use abrasive chemicals to clean the Mac as they will scratch the body. I use a can of compressed air to blow out dust in the inside of my Mac.

Keep a maintenance schedule

Since we are keeping track of several maintenance tasks, there are two things you can do to remind yourself. One is to print out the following chart, Table 1.1 and place it on the wall in front of your Mac. The second method is to log onto **http://www.MemoToMe. com/**.

This Web site is a personal reminder service where you can create recurring daily, weekly, or monthly reminders that will send you e-mail to remind you of the tasks.

Table 1.1 Mac Maintenance Schedule

Chore	Daily	Weekly	Monthly	3-6 Months
Back up files	x			
Zap PRAM				x
Rebuild Desktop			x	
Virus Check (on downloads)	x	x		
Clean Mac		x		
Run Disk First Aid or Norton's		x		
Defrag (Optimize)				x

2

Common Mac Ailments

In Chapter 1, you learned how to avoid certain potential problems that can occur in your G3 Macintosh by using preventive medicine. This chapter explains those problems and others. Even the best-made machines can break. The Mac is no exception. The troubleshooting guide in Chapter Four is designed to walk you through potential hardware problems. This chapter deals with common software problems like system freeze, extension conflicts, and corrupted software. For new Mac owners, having your Mac screen freeze on startup, or seeing a dialog box with a System Error and the Bomb, can be frightening. However, most software problems on your Mac can be corrected easily.

Over the years there have been a few recurring problems for Mac users. This chapter will describe them and tell you what to do to recover, or steps to take to avoid getting them in the future.

Recovering from a Freeze

Often a simple restart will take care of the problem if your Mac screen freezes or you get the dialog box with a System Error and the Bomb.

Simultaneously depress the **Command (Apple)-Option-ESC** keys, which should quit the program and bring you back to the desktop. You will loose whatever work you had, however. If this does not work, you have to force restart your computer.

Perform a force restart by depressing the **Command (Apple)-Control-Keyboard Power Button** combo. This works most of the time. It doesn't work in the first release of the Mac.

For the owners of the Mac Model A, the recommended way to restart your computer is to take a paper clip and insert it in the reset hole located between the modem and Ethernet ports on the right side of your Mac. That doesn't always work either.

The easiest way is to take your right hand and pull out the power plug on the right backside of the computer. Plug it back in, wait 30 seconds, and hit the power key on your keyboard. Unfortunately you lose your work when you do this. Many software programs like WordPerfect and MS Word perform an automatic backup periodically so you may lose only a small amount of information instead of all of it. Count on the worst case.

Most of the common crashes on your Mac are due to faulty software. A crash can be caused by extension conflicts, incorrect software drivers for your hard drive, printer, or other peripheral, or a corrupt preference file, or even your system software.

Corrupted Preference Files

In the system folder is another folder called "Preferences." It contains many folders and files. Preference files are specific files married to applications and are important for your software to work correctly. However, not all preferences are stored in this folder. Some software programs keep their preference files in the same folder as the application itself.

Preference files keep track of a program's "preferences": what information may be regularly used, such as storing the phone number for a bulletin board you visit regularly, or making sure your desktop is a certain color, or a certain font is always used. Often you set the preferences yourself or the software program does it as a matter of tracking what you do.

Every time you change a setting, the corresponding preference file will be updated or a new one created. Sometimes a preference file will get corrupted and cause the parent application to perform strangely.

There is a simple solution for correcting a corrupted preference file. If you suspect that a preference file is the problem, throw it in the trash and empty the trash can (make sure the application it belongs to is closed before you do the procedure). When you restart your computer, the software program will create a new preference file. Because you tossed the old one, you may have to reset your software settings since the old settings are now deleted.

What happens if that doesn't work? You see a dialog box that says the file is in use and you can't delete it. I've taken the preference file out of the system folder altogether and placed it elsewhere on the hard drive, then restarted my Mac. This will create a new preference file and you can then toss the old one in the trash. If that doesn't work, then you need to reinstall the application software, which will overwrite the old preference file.

When the Finder's preference file becomes corrupted, restart your Mac from the system CD-ROM that comes bundled with it. Hold the "C" key down when restarting to make the CD the startup disc. Drag the Finder Preference file from the CD-ROM over to your system folder on the hard drive. A dialog box will inform you that there is a preexisting file but just click **ok**.

Bad Drivers

Your Mac interfaces with third-party peripherals like scanners, digital cameras, drawing pads, printers, hard drives, and the like through special software programs called drivers. Every time Apple releases a new update of the system software there is new driver software for the hard drive. However, there is no guarantee that the new software and drivers will work with all those third party drivers. This could cause problems.

Before you update the new system software and Apple's drivers, check with the vendors of all your peripherals and see if they have new drivers that will work with the new Apple software. You can then download them from their Web sites and install them. Of course you can also update the Apple drivers and see if everything works beforehand.

If you're using a hard drive that is not an Apple hard drive, perhaps a second external hard drive for backup, then you must use that third-party's driver software. While it is possible to overwrite the hard drive with Apple's drivers (with version 1.3 or better), it is strongly suggested that you do not do so.

Clock Not Keeping the Right Time?

If you find that preferences like desktop color change, or your clock is keeping the wrong time or date, you may have a problem with your Parameter Random Access Memory (PRAM), a tiny amount of memory that is continually on and is powered by a small battery on your Mac. PRAM maintains information on things that you don't want to keep setting, like background color, video settings, network information, time of day, and such. It can get corrupted and crash your computer.

You reset (zap) the PRAM to restore it to the original factory settings and clear out the problem. However, since the PRAM resets the Mac to the factory settings for many control panels like General Controls, Keyboard, Startup Disk, Mouse, and Map, you need to go back and reset them to your liking.

To zap the PRAM, choose restart, or when you boot up your Mac hold the **Command Option-P-R** keys and wait till you hear the startup tone at least twice. Go back to your Control Panels and reset them.

Computer acting funny

If you have tried every other fix and your computer is still doing funny things, you could have a computer virus. There are only a few viruses in the Mac community but enough to keep you on the alert. You should purchase a commercial or shareware virus detector and use it frequently. Chances are you will never get a virus but it is better to be safe than sorry.

Subscribe to the Mac Virus mailing list to keep informed of new viruses. This list announces viruses on the Mac.

To subscribe, send e-mail to:
listproc@listproc. bgsu.edu
In the body of the message, type:
subscribe mac-virus-announce YOUR FULL NAME
There are several good virus detectors on the market. Make sure you install all new updates as they become available.

Dead Batteries

Some day you will start your Mac and the date will have reverted to August 27, 1956 or January 1, 1904, or the monitor will turn black, or your Chooser settings will not stay set and have to be reset every day you start up. Those are the signs that your onboard battery is weak or dead. Batteries don't last forever, but the problem is easily fixed. Replace the dead battery with a fresh one and zap the PRAM by restarting and holding down the **CMD-OPT-P-R** keys.

You must be careful with installing batteries since they can explode if you put them in wrong. Apple recommends you have an Apple authorized agent do it for you.

EBatts.com (**http://www.eBatts.com**) is a Web site that sells almost every conceivable type of battery. It also has a great section on explaining the various types of batteries, how to install them, etc. Visit the Macintosh Battery Page at **http://www.academ.com/info/Macintosh/** for more information on Mac batteries.

Extension Conflicts

The Mac operating system has the ability to add mini applications or helper files during startup that improve the productivity of the Mac operating system. These files are known as extensions and Control Panels. Both are automatically installed when you power up your Mac (you see them run along the bottom of your screen). They load into memory. Extensions, also called *inits*, are preconfigured so you just install them; they are already trained in what to do. On the other hand, Control Panels allow you to set certain functions. Examples of these are virus checkers, a calculator, date and time, etc.

If you have a lot of extensions, one or two may compete for the same place and cause your Mac to act funny, or not even boot up properly. Often this will happen right after you install a new software program. The new extension conflicts with a preexisting one (or vice versa), or the problem may strike when your are in the middle of writing something important.

If it happens immediately after installing a new program, that's a clue that it *probably* is the new program's extension. You can turn off all extensions when you power up your Mac. Hold down the **Shift** key while you restart. This turns off all extensions and your Mac should boot up, although some of the functions will be disabled.

To continue troubleshooting the problem go under the Apple Menu, in the Control Panels section, and select Extensions Manager. This is a control panel from Apple that lets you turn on and off extensions, and create special sets of extensions.

Look for the new extension that was just installed and deselect it by clicking on the checkbox to the left, then restart the Mac. If it powers up correctly, then the problem is your new extension. If it still does not boot up correctly, go back to the Extensions Manager and select the "Base" option. This is the minimum number of extensions needed to start your machine. If the Mac does not start up after that, you may have to perform a clean install of the system software or conduct a labor intensive trial-and-error search.

Trial and error includes moving all the extensions out of their folders, and then adding one or two back at a time then restarting. You continue to move files in and out until the Mac fails to restart; by then you know the name of the culprit.

Hold down the **Option** key while restarting the Mac. If your machine continues to start up and makes it to the desktop, go into your System folder. Find the Extension folder and grab the new extension file and take it out of the System folder. Restart the machine. If it starts up fine, you know the file was the problem.

Since the conflict can be the order in which the extensions are loading, you can try to rearrange the order. Click on the new extension to highlight it. You will notice the area where the name is located becomes highlighted and you can insert a new name, or in our case, just place a space before the name by inserting your cursor in front of the first letter and hitting the space bar. Then restart. If the Mac loads fine then the problem is solved. If not, you may have to do a clean install of the system software as mentioned previously, or contact the third-party company and see if they have a software update.

If you do indeed have a conflicting extension and you need it for the software to work, contact the software company, or check their Web site to see if they have a newer version. This is a must if you upgraded your system software to a newer version. The software company may not have had time to release an update, or even know it conflicted with the newer system software. It's wise to wait a month or two after a new system software update comes to market. You can read about the problem files from others who did not wait. Avoid the hassles if you can.

Over an extended period of time you will collect a lot of extensions. There is a program called Extension Overload (**www.mir.com.my/~cmteng**) that you can download or read online. This program contains a listing of all the system extensions and control panels that you can, or will, find in the System folder of every Macintosh. The program lists them by name and explains what they do. This allows you to decide whether to keep a certain control panel or extension. Extension Overload also lists Mac error codes.

You can avoid a lot of these extension conflict hassles by purchasing Conflict Catcher by Casady & Greene (**http://www.casadyg.com**). Its sole purpose is to make your computer avoid system conflicts. Conflict Catcher describes and lets you manage thousands (3,900+) of files from everyday startup files to plug-ins and filters, and if you do have a problem with your system, it determines which files are causing problems on your machine.

Files No Longer Launching When Clicking on Them

Sometimes you will see a file you saved has lost its icon or when you double click on it, the parent application does not launch it. For example, you wrote a letter to a friend using Microsoft Word but when you restart the Mac, the file has a generic look, there is no Microsoft icon.

There is an invisible file, the Desktop File, a database that keeps track of icons and what applications created them, but once in a while it loses track of one or two. You can restore these files by rebuilding the desktop. When you start up the Mac, simply hold down the **Command** and **Option** keys. A dialog box will ask you if are sure you want to perform the operation and you will. Select the **OK** button. It will take a few minutes if you have a lot of files.

Flashing Question Mark

Some day you may start up your Mac and see the dreaded flashing question mark on your monitor. Nothing appears. If you back up your data every day then it's nothing more than a mere inconvenience. If you don't back up everyday, a sense of panic sweeps over you.

Most of the time the problem arises when your system software gets corrupted and a system reinstall will do the fix. Place your Mac Install CD-ROM into the CD-ROM drive, hold down the **C** key and reboot, then reinstall the system software. Do a regular, not fresh, install first.

If the hard drive appears after you boot up with the CD-ROM, take the System, Finder, and Finder Preference files from the hard drive's System folder and trash them (empty the trash). Then take the System, Finder, and Finder Preferences file from the CD-ROM boot-up disc and drag them over to the system folder on the hard drive. That usually works as a temporary fix. If it doesn't, then do a complete reinstall.

If nothing works, you need to use a disk recovery program. There are several on the market to recover crashed disks and files. One of the most popular recovery programs is Norton Disk Utilities from Symantec (**http://www.symantec.com**). It can recover hard drives, floppies, Zips, and even separate files by themselves. I recommend it.

Disk First Aid, Apple's recovery system, comes on your Mac, and automatically goes into action if your Mac is turned off without powering down, or crashes. You can periodically run the program to keep your hard drive in good working order. I like to give it a spin about once a week. There are other third-party drive and disk recovery programs like Data Rescue, DiskWarrior, MacMedic, Norton Utilities for Macintosh, and TechTool Pro 2.

Be sure the product works on the Mac and system version you have.

Mac Is Slow Starting Up or Slow Operating

If you have a lot of RAM installed on your Mac, there is a RAM test performed when you first start up, so it is normal to have a smiling Mac face for a while as those tests are performed. Moreover, if you have more than the normal complement of Extensions and Control Panels, it will take a while to load them at startup.

If you see more than one row of icons running across the bottom of your screen when you start up, you have too many. Do you really need them all? Are you using Virtual memory? Open up the Memory control panel and turn it off.

Calculate Folder Size may be on. Select **View Options** from the View menu while the window is active and uncheck Calculate Folder Size.

Turn File sharing off. Open up the File Sharing Control Panel. Click on the **Stop** button next to File Sharing.

Easy G3 Upgrades You Can Do Yourself!

Apple has made it quite easy to perform a number of upgrades to your G3 computer. Adding memory, Video RAM, expansion cards, modems, even hard drives can be performed without having to take the computer into a shop. Of course you run the risk of causing serious damage to your computer if you do perform the work yourself and do not take proper precautions.

Do not use any tools that are magnetic, such as a screwdriver with magnetic tip. Always wear an antistatic wrist band and frequently touch any metal part of the computer such as the expansion card chassis, or hard drive carrier, when you are working, to discharge any static you may have built up. Do not shuffle your feet, get up and walk around, or move in a way that may build up an electric charge. Give yourself plenty of time to finish any upgrade you start. Do not start then try to finish later.

The best and most assured upgrade path is to bring your G3 to an Apple certified technician. You should also carry an AppleCare warranty in case your G3 computer has a serious hardware failure—one which you cannot fix regardless of your level of expertise.

The following upgrades are easy upgrades that you can perform yourself given reasonable care as outlined above.

iMac Memory Upgrade

Apple has made it easy to upgrade your RAM, giving you the opportunity to have over 500MB of memory using third-party memory upgrades. Apple recommends that you have a certified technician install memory since your warranty will be voided if you damage your computer. If you decide to do it yourself, be sure to wear an anti-static wrist protector and do not use any power or magnetic tools. All you need is a plain Phillips-head screwdriver.

Important Note: On earlier iMac models (A, B, and C), memory modules (RAM) must be of the SDRAM SODIMM type whereas the DV models require the PC100 type. They don't mix!

Installing RAM on early iMac models (233-266 333 MHz)

Installing upper slot memory into your iMac

STEP ONE
Unplug all the cables from the computer, including the power cord, phone cable, keyboard or other USB devices. There should be no cabling anywhere connected to the computer.

Place a piece of foam, or a soft towel or cloth on the surface where you will doing the upgrade. Be sure you have plenty of room to work and that it is clean and flat. Hold the handle with one hand and the front of the computer with the other and slowly tilt and place the Mac on the foam or protective cover so that the underside of the iMac is facing you.

STEP TWO

Use a Phillips screwdriver to unscrew the screw on the lower back cover.

Remove this screw and set it aside.

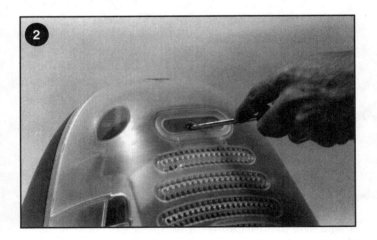

STEP THREE

Grab the small plastic handle on the cover and pull the cover away from the computer. Place the cover with the screw.

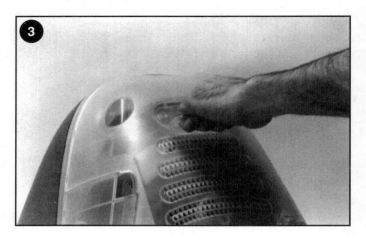

STEP FOUR

Place your hand or fingers on any exposed metal on the logic board/drive assembly (wear an anti-static wristband). This will discharge any static electricity and help protect the computer from damage caused by an electrostatic discharge.

Apple recommends that you do this always before you touch any parts, or install any components, anytime you are inside the computer. Do not walk around the room or shuffle your feet while you are working on the computer. This could generate static. Be sure that when you are about to start the process of upgrading you have sufficient time to finish the project. For example, don't start just before dinner, or going to work.

Touch the metal part of the logic board/drive assembly computer as shown.

STEP FIVE

Use a Phillips screwdriver to unscrew the two screws inside the plastic handle.

If your computer has clamps over any cables, release the cables underneath the clamp. If the clamp has a screw, unscrew it first, then release the cable. On some iMac models there is a third screw that needs to be removed on the left side of the assembly.

STEP SIX

You will use a screwdriver to disconnect the video cable. Disconnect the remaining cables connected to the main logic board.

STEP SEVEN

Move the disconnected cables out of the way.

STEP EIGHT

Place one hand on the plastic handle, and with the other hold the cables out of the way.

Gently pull the handle straight up and out of the computer.

Lay the logic board/drive on a flat clean surface. Touch the assembly to discharge any static you may have built up.

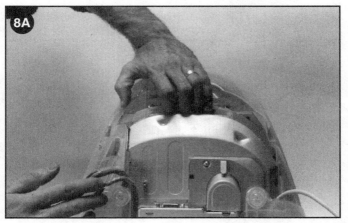

STEP NINE

Grab the metal shield at the ends, as shown. Snap it off by lifting both sides. Place it next to the other removed parts.

STEP TEN

Take a DIMM you want to install, by the edges only, and slide it into the slot at an angle. The DIMM has a notch in it so it will only fit one way into the slot so you don't have to worry about putting it in wrong.

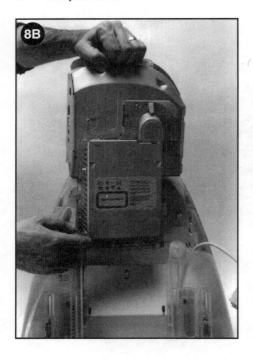

STEP ELEVEN

Push down the DIMM with your thumb. It will snap in and lie flat and parallel to the logic board.

If that is all you will be installing, snap the metal shield back into place and continue to the section on iMac Assembly below. If you are going to install memory in the lower slot or VRAM, continue.

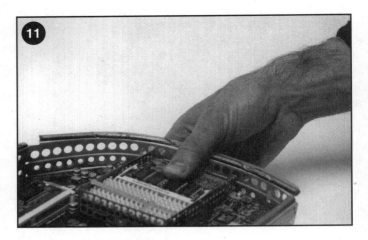

**Installing lower slot memory into
your iMac**

Note: If you install lower slot memory in your iMac
(early models) this voids your Apple Warranty.

STEP ONE

With a single-edge screwdriver, carefully remove and
pry the retaining clip out that goes across the heat
sink.

STEP TWO

Use the clip to remove the heat sink. **Note:** *Do not* touch the heat sink as it may be hot if you just turned off your iMac.

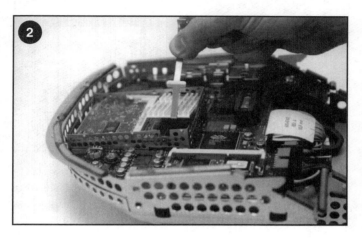

STEP THREE

Using the clip again, put it in the back of the processor card and pry it up gently to remove the card.

Grab the card by the edges only and remove it.

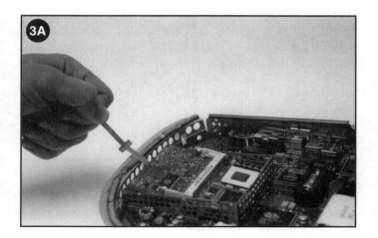

STEP FOUR

Flip the card over to expose the lower slot. Use your thumbs to pry open and outward the retaining clips that hold the DIMM in the slot. This will pop up the DIMM.

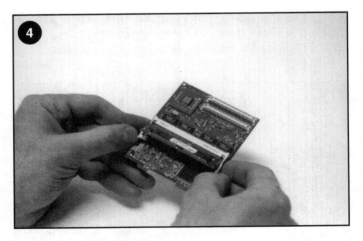

STEP FIVE

Take out the old DIMM and install the new DIMM. Line up the notch on the DIMM to the slot, inserting it in an angle so it is seated.

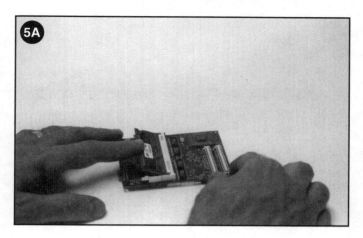

Push down the card gently until you hear it snap into the connectors. Use firm and even pressure.

STEP SIX

Reinstall the processor card into the iMac. Notice the two tabs on the front. Line up the board with the tabs on front and the logic board connector on the other end.

Insert the card into the tab slots and gently press the card back into the connector.

STEP SEVEN

Replace the heat sink clip and heat sink.

STEP EIGHT

Replace the metal cage.

If you are through go to the section on iMac assembly. If you are upgrading the Video RAM (on the 233 model) go to the next section.

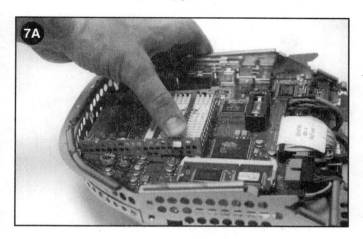

Upgrading the Video RAM

The earliest 233 MHz model of the iMac came with 2 MB of VRAM, expandable to 8. Models 266 (B) and 333 (C) came with 8 MB already installed. To upgrade the 233 MHz model, continue.

STEP ONE
Locate the VRAM slot to the left of the processor board, as shown.

Step Two

Remove the old video RAM module by spreading the connectors and pulling the module out.

Step Three

Install the new VRAM module at an angle into the slot using the notch as a guide. Handle the DIMM by the sides not the connectors. Lightly push the module down until it snaps into place and is lying flat.

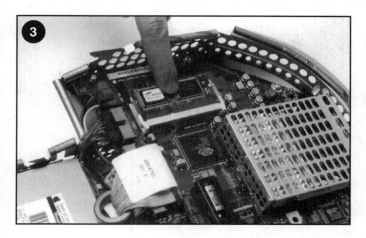

iMac assembly

Inspect your work and make sure nothing is lying inside your logic board, and that you have put everything back again as you found it.

STEP ONE
Take one hand and grab the plastic handle; have the other hand holding the bottom, and gently lower the logic board/drive straight down into the computer, into the plastic slides, until it is in place. Two tabs must go behind the plastic slides. Be sure all cables are out of the way when you do this.

STEP TWO
Reach under the front of the iMac while you are guiding the logic board into the computer and make sure the CD bezel is guided into the front opening to insure proper fit and alignment.

STEP THREE
Reconnect all cables. If your iMac has clamps over any cables, reconnect them. If the clamp has a screw, screw the clamp into place. Be sure to screw in the video cable if it is needed.

STEP FOUR

Reconnect the two screws into the handle.

STEP FIVE

Replace the plastic cover. It should snap back into place around all of the edges. If it does not fit properly, a cable may not be secured correctly.

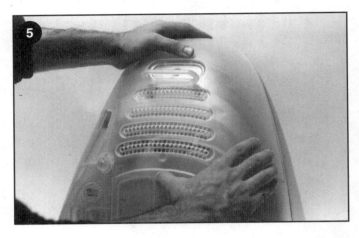

STEP SIX

Screw the single screw between the plastic handle back on the lower back cover using a Phillips screwdriver.

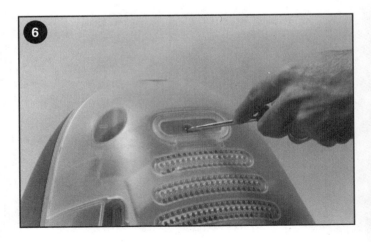

STEP SEVEN

Reconnect all the cables and power cord and restart the computer to make sure everything is working fine. Look under the Apple Menu "About This Computer" and see that the new memory increase is registered in the "Built In Memory" item. You can also view this information using the Apple System Profiler in the Apple Menu.

Installing RAM into the iMac DV models

Apple went out of its way to make installing RAM into the new DV modems a piece of cake.

STEP ONE

Unplug all the cables from the computer, including the power cord, phone cable, keyboard or other USB devices. There should be no cabling anywhere connected to the computer.

Place a piece of foam, or a soft towel or cloth on the surface where you will doing the upgrade. Be sure you have plenty of room to work and that it is clean and flat. Hold the handle with one hand and the front of the computer with the other and slowly tilt it and place it on the foam or protective cover so that the underside of the iMac is facing you.

Step Two
Take a quarter and insert it into the slot.

Turn it counterclockwise.

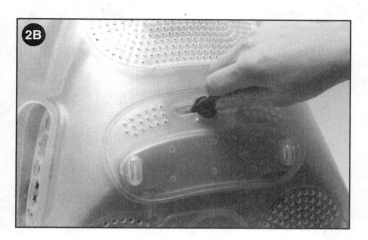

Grab the lid with your fingers.

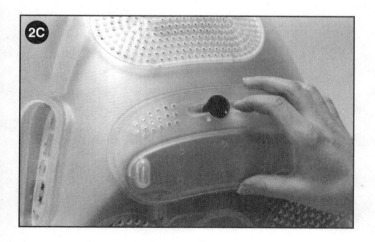

Pull the lid off. It drops down.

Locate the empty DIMM slot (on the bottom) or remove the DIMM already in the computer by spreading the white tabs apart and lifting out the DIMM.

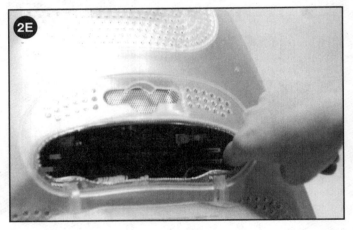

Line up the new DIMM so that the notches on the DIMM line up with their counterparts on the DIMM slot.

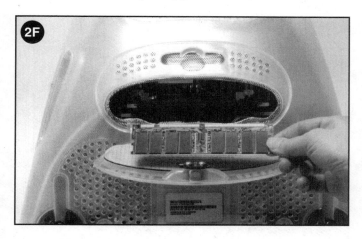

Holding the edges, push the DIMM into the slot firmly until it snaps into place.

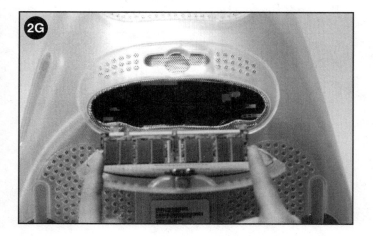

Be sure tabs are together.

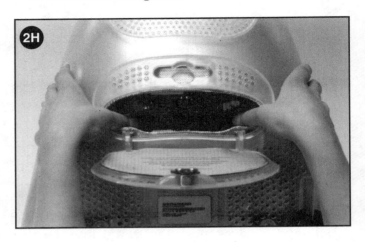

Reinstall the plastic plate.

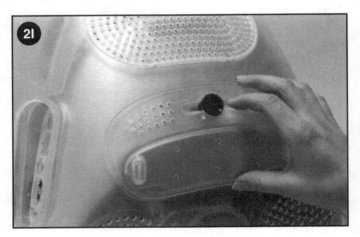

Insert the quarter into the slot.

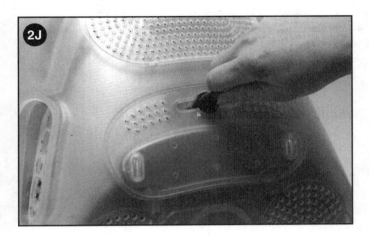

Turn it clockwise to lock the plate into place.

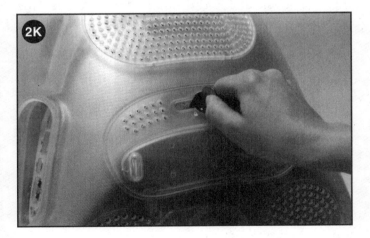

You have just completed installation.

Reconnect all the cables and the power cord and restart the computer to make sure everything is working fine. Look under the Apple Menu "About This Computer" and see that the new memory increase is registered in the "Built In Memory" item. You can also view this information using the Apple System Profiler in the Apple Menu.

Installing a hard drive into your iMac 233-266-333

While chances are you will never have to remove or replace your built-in hard drive, there is a great step-by-step tutorial on doing it on the Web site. **http://www.theimac.com/drive_steps.shtml**. Replacing the hard drive is a bit difficult but can be done.

Installing a SCSI card into your iMac 233 MHz Revision A or B

You can install a SCSI card on your old iMac but it's not easy. The Web site above has a good discussion about it, where you can buy it, and detailed step-by-step instructions. Go to **http://www.theimac.com/ imac_scsi/scsi_card.shtml**.

G3 Desktop Upgrade

Installing RAM on G3 desktop model

Note: Be sure to discharge any static electricity by touching the metal PCI port covers in the back of the computer before you start working (wear an anti-static wrist strap). Do not walk around the room or shuffle your feet while upgrading. If you cannot complete the upgrade at one time, wait until you have the time.

STEP ONE
Unplug all the cables from the computer, including the power cord, phone cable, keyboard, or other SCSI devices. There should be no cabling anywhere connected to the computer.

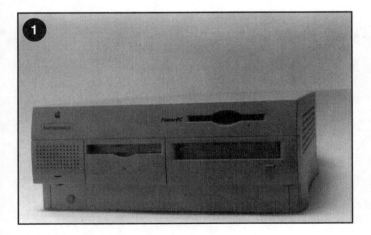

STEP TWO
Take your thumbs and place them on the buttons on the bottom of the front panel, and your fingers on top of the case. Press the buttons in, to release the cover.

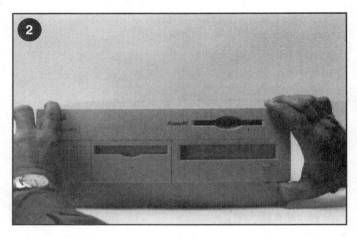

STEP THREE
Slide the cover forward and up exposing the inside of
the computer. The EMI shields in front will probably
fall out as well. Put these aside.

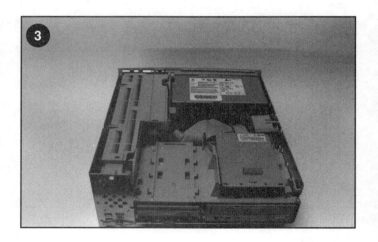

STEP FOUR
Place two fingers as shown on the expansion card
cover to the left of the power supply.

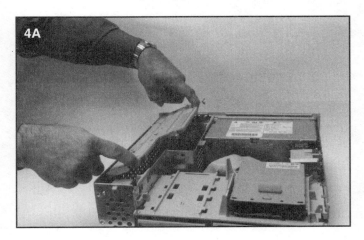

Lift this cover up and back.

STEP FIVE

Slide the two beige buttons (release switches) toward the center.

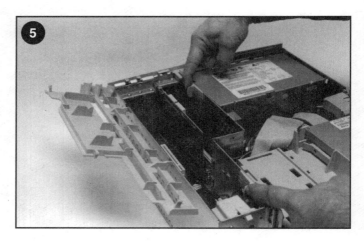

STEP SIX

Grab the metal tab in the middle and pull it up. Make sure the plastic support arm is down, which braces the assembly (it fits in the hole on the bottom) and a little foot in which the assembly sits on.

STEP SEVEN

Locate the three RAM slots and spread the clips (Apple calls them ejectors) open. There may be one or two of these clips.

STEP EIGHT
Line up the notches on the DIMM with the DIMM slot
and apply equal pressure with thumbs as you place
the DIMM in the slot. The DIMM should snap into
place.

STEP NINE
Grab the assembly with one hand. With the other,
grab the retaining clip that was holding it up and pull

up, then slowly move the assembly back down into place. This prevents the clip from getting broken. Pop the little foot back in place.

STEP TEN
Take the beige buttons (release switches) and push them out to lock.

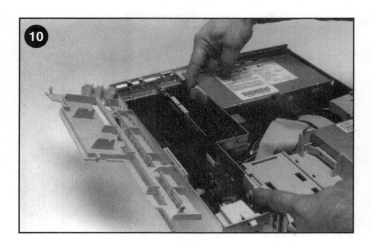

STEP ELEVEN
Place the expansion card cover back down.

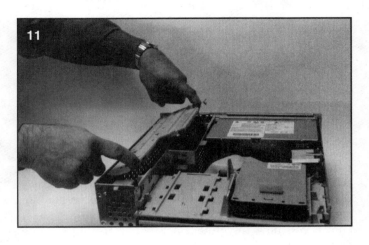

STEP TWELVE
Slide the cover back onto the computer in a down and backward motion making sure the two buttons in front lock into place.

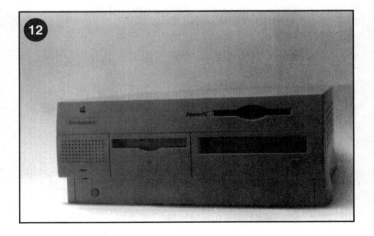

Reconnect all the cables and power cord and restart the computer to make sure everything is working fine. Look under the Apple Menu "About This Computer" and see that the new memory increase is registered in the "Built In Memory" item. You can also view this information using the Apple System Profiler in the Apple Menu.

Adding a SCSI hard drive on G3 desktop model

Some early versions of the G3 Desktop were shipped with a SCSI hard drive, while most have IDE drives. You can have both in your G3. There is a built-in SCSI connector on the logic board and you can also add a third-party PCI SCSI card, allowing you to connect many SCSI peripherals to your Mac. This section shows you how to connect a SCSI hard drive. Apple removed the SCSI connection on the Power Macintosh G3 (Blue and White) and Macintosh Server G3 systems and replaced it with FireWire. Apple offers the Ultra SCSI PCI card so you can connect to those existing external SCSI peripherals you might have, such as scanners, tape drives, and hard disks that use standard SCSI (SCSI-1), Fast SCSI (SCSI-2), and Ultra SCSI (also called Ultra Narrow SCSI).

Note: Be sure to discharge any static electricity by touching the metal PCI port covers in the back of the computer, or the power supply, before you start working (wear an anti-static wristband). Do not walk around the room or shuffle your feet while upgrading. If you cannot complete the upgrade at one time, wait until you have the time.

STEP ONE

Unplug all the cables from the computer, including the power cord, phone cable, keyboard or other SCSI devices. There should be no cabling anywhere connected to the computer.

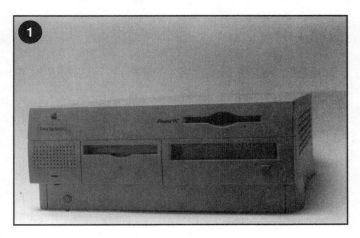

STEP TWO

Take your thumbs and place them on buttons on the bottom of the front panel, and your fingers on top of the case. Press the buttons in to release the cover.

STEP THREE

Slide the cover forward and up exposing the inside of the computer. The EMI shields in front will probably fall out as well. Put these aside.

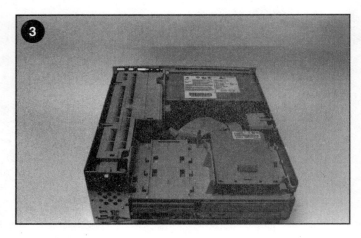

STEP FOUR

Locate the expansion bay to the left of the floppy drive.

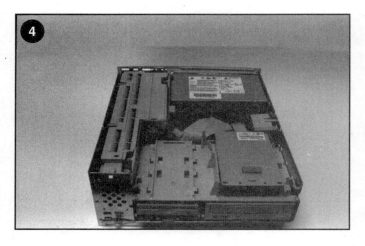

STEP FIVE

Connect the SCSI cable to the SCSI connector as shown and run up to the expansion bay. Connect the power cable to the hard drive.

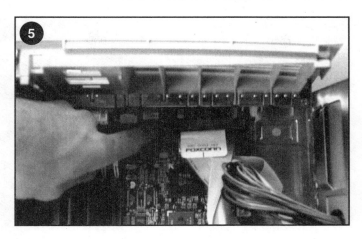

STEP SIX

Connect the SCSI cable and power cable to the hard drive. If the hard drive is not connected to a cage, install this before you place it in the bay. Be sure that the hard drive has a unique SCSI ID.

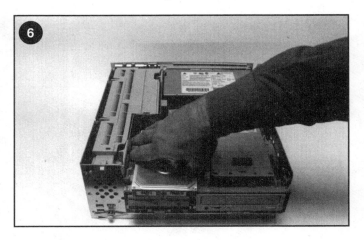

STEP SEVEN

Slide the cover back onto the computer in a down and backward motion making sure the two buttons in front lock into place.

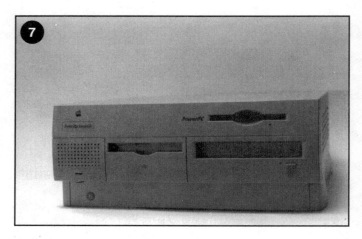

G3 Beige Minitower (or Server) Upgrade

Installing RAM on G3 minitower (beige) model

STEP ONE

Turn the Minitower to its left side and push the green button on the cover. Pull down and out. The panel comes completely off.

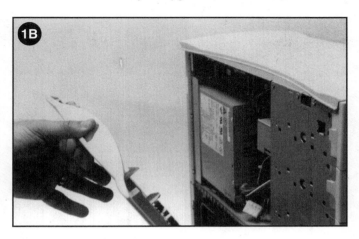

STEP TWO
Place the minitower on its side so that the exposed computer is facing up.

STEP THREE
Find the two green tabs and pull them up.

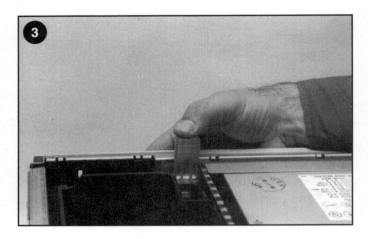

STEP FOUR
Insert one hand in the black handle and lift up.

STEP FIVE
Locate three DIMM slots.

Spread the white tabs apart before you insert DIMM.

STEP SIX

Take the DIMM by the edges and slowly but firmly press them into the DIMM slots until you hear them snap into place.

If you are done, go to Step Seven.

Upgrading or replacing the video RAM

Note: To the left of the DIMM slots is the video RAM. If you need to replace it or upgrade it, you may need to take out the sound card next to it first, then proceed.

To remove the existing SGRAM DIMM, slightly spread the arms of video memory slot apart and the SGRAM DIMM will snap up. Take it out and align the new DIMM with its notches to the slot. The DIMM can only go in one way. Press the DIMM into the slot

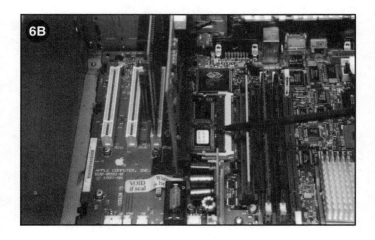

and it will snap into place lying flat and parallel to the logic board.

STEP SEVEN
Grab black handle on chassis and place back.

STEP EIGHT
Lock the two green latches.

STEP NINE
Place the side panel back on.

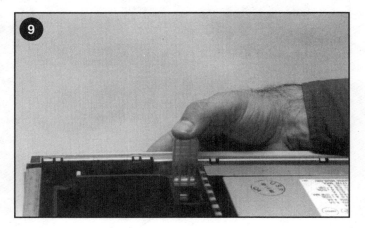

G3 Blue & White Minitower (or Server) Upgrade

Installing RAM on G3 blue and white model

Note: Be sure to discharge any static electricity by touching the metal PCI port covers in the back of the computer before you start working (wear an anti-static wristband). Do not walk around the room or shuffle your feet while upgrading. If you cannot complete the upgrade at one time, wait until you have the time.

STEP ONE
Turn the Minitower to its right side and grab the latch and lift up.

STEP TWO
Pull the unit down so it rests on the flat surface.

STEP THREE
Notice that you have easy access to most of the
computer.

STEP FOUR
Locate the four DIMM slots as shown.

STEP FIVE
Spread the white DIMM slot latches apart with your fingers.

STEP SIX

Handle the DIMMs by the edges and seat them firmly in the DIMM slots at an angle.

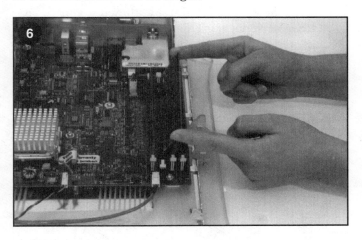

STEP SEVEN

Firmly push down evenly on the DIMM module until it snaps into place.

If you are through, go to the section on assembly. If not, continue.

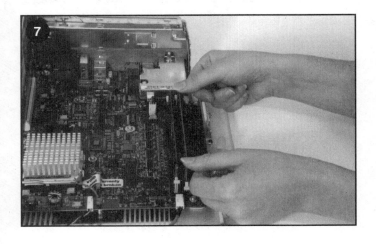

Installing a PCI card in the G3 blue and white model

You can add PCI cards to your Mac, increasing the versatility of your computer by allowing you to connect other peripherals. This exercise shows you how to connect a PCI card within minutes.

STEP ONE
With your Mac open and lying flat, locate the three PCI slots to the left.

STEP TWO
Using a Phillips head screwdriver, unscrew the port access cover.

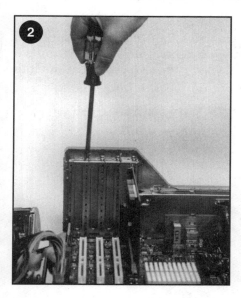

STEP THREE
Lift and remove the port access cover.

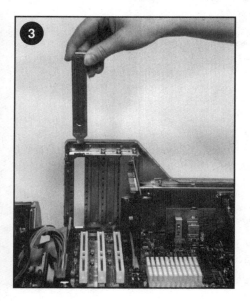

STEP FOUR

Remove the PCI card and handle it from the sides. Do not touch any of the connectors or electronic components on the card. Look for the connector that fits into the expansion slot.

STEP FIVE

Insert the card into the expansion slot and firmly apply equal pressure to seat the card. Be sure it's seated evenly.

STEP SIX

Reinstall the screw on top to secure the card in place.

STEP SEVEN

Close the computer unless you are going to add another peripheral.

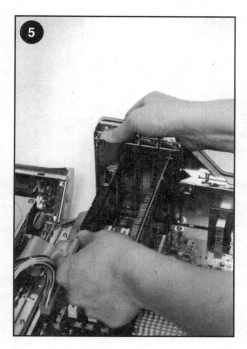

Installing a modem in the G3 blue and white model

Note: Be sure to discharge any static electricity by touching the metal PCI port covers in the back of the computer before you start working (wear an anti-static wristband). Do not walk around the room or shuffle your feet while upgrading. If you cannot complete the upgrade at one time, wait until you have the time.

STEP ONE

Turn the computer so that the back is facing you. Notice where the modem port is located. It has a picture of a telephone.

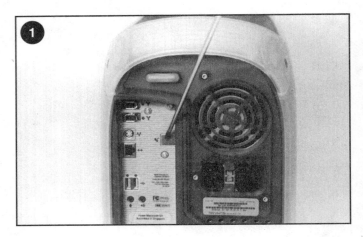

Step Two
Turn the Minitower to its right side and grab the latch and lift up.

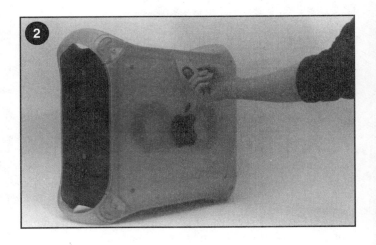

Step Three
Pull the unit down so it rests on the flat surface.

STEP FOUR

Turn it so the back of the computer is facing you and remove the screw below the modem port (to the right of it). Take out the modem plug.

STEP FIVE

Take the modem by its side and align it with the modem port.

STEP SIX

Angle the modem so that the right side goes into the slot first and then straighten it out as it snaps into place.

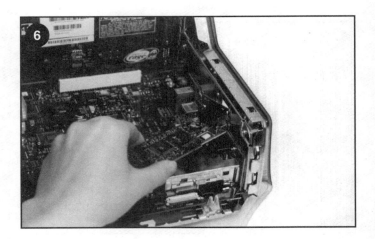

STEP SEVEN

With one hand holding the modem firmly on the back, reattach the screw on the right side of the modem port on the outside of the back panel.

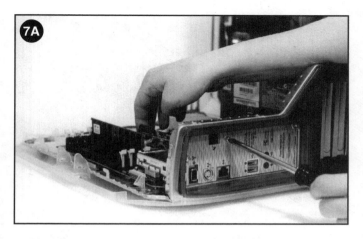

There may be another screw on the inside that attaches the modem to the logic board. Locate the cable connection at the bottom.

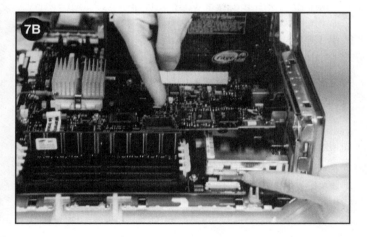

STEP EIGHT
Attach the modem cable to the modem and logic board.

STEP NINE
Close the computer.

Installing a SCSI hard drive in the G3 blue and white model

If your computer came with only an ATA hard drive, you need to add a SCSI expansion card (see above) but you can add additional SCSI drives internally or externally using the card.

Note: Be sure to discharge any static electricity by touching the metal PCI port covers in the back of the computer before you start working (wear an anti-static wristband). Do not walk around the room or shuffle your feet while upgrading. If you cannot complete the upgrade at one time, wait until you have the time.

STEP ONE
Turn the Minitower to its right side and grab the latch and lift up.

Step Two
Pull the unit down so it rests on the flat surface.

Step Three
Locate the bundled power cable and the ribbon cable on the logic board.

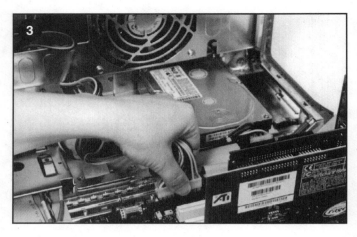

STEP FOUR
Unplug the power cable by pulling up.

STEP FIVE
Locate the ribbon cable that was to the right of the power cable.

STEP SIX
Remove the ribbon cable by pulling up.

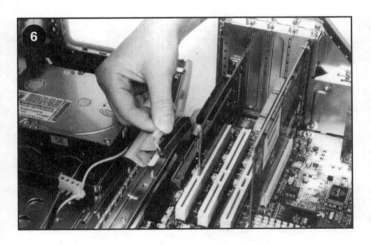

STEP SEVEN
Remove the screw that is located at the rear of the
drive carrier.

STEP EIGHT
Lift off the retaining clip.

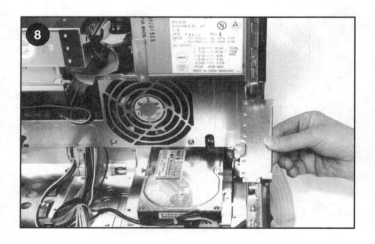

STEP NINE
Find the power cable attached to drive on the carrier.
Disconnect the power cable and any other cables con-
nected on the carrier.

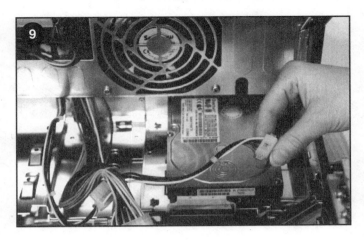

STEP TEN
Lift the carrier at the rear and slide it out.

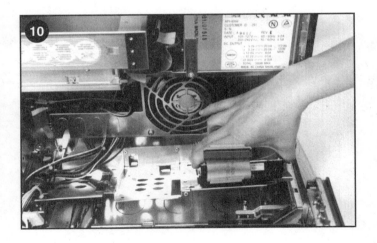

STEP ELEVEN
Notice where the cables came through the drive carrier so you can reinsert them later.

STEP TWELVE
Lay the drive carrier down in front of you.

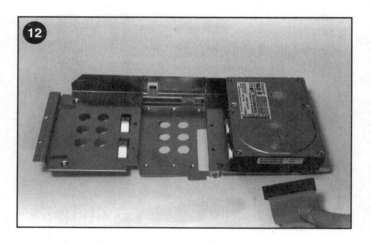

STEP THIRTEEN
Give the new SCSI drive a unique SCSI ID before you
put it in. See your manufacturer's manual on locating
the ID block. According to Apple, if the Mac came with
one Ultra2 LVD SCSI drive, it has SCSI ID 0. If it
came with two drives, they have IDs 0 and 1. If it has

a third factory-installed drive this has the ID 2. The SCSI PCI card has the ID 7. The drive in position 1 is the startup drive.

Insert the drive on the drive carrier.

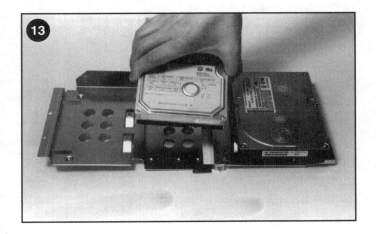

STEP FOURTEEN
Screw the drive into the carrier.

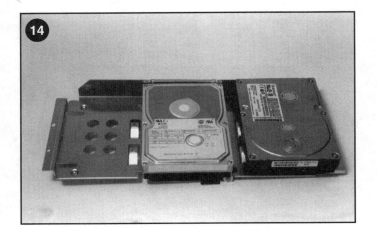

STEP FIFTEEN

Attach the cables to the drives and through the carrier.

STEP SIXTEEN

Reattach the drive carrier onto the computer, watching that you don't break or crimp any cables, and screw the retaining clip back on. Attach the cable from the first drive back to its connector.

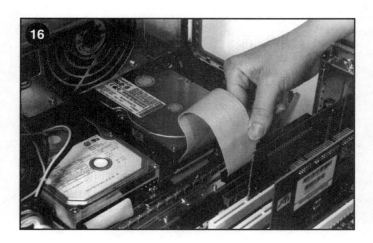

STEP SEVENTEEN

Attach the power cables and ribbon cables to their respective connectors (SCSI and ATA are different types so you can't make a mistake).

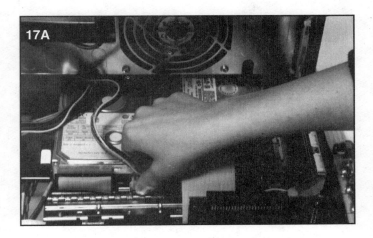

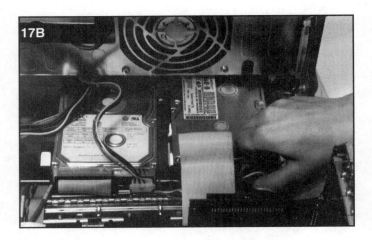

If you added a SCSI drive and your Mac came with an ATA drive, attach the main power cable bundle and

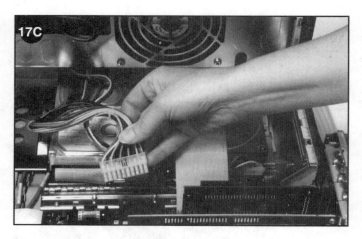

the ATA ribbon cable to the main logic board and the SCSI ribbon cable to the SCSI PCI card.

If you added a SCSI drive and your Mac already came with one or two SCSI drives, attach the main power cable bundle to the main logic board and the SCSI ribbon cable to the SCSI PCI card.

STEP EIGHTEEN
Close the computer panel.

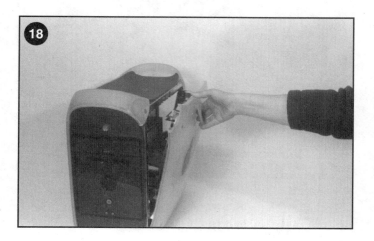

iBook Memory Upgrade

Apple has made upgrading the memory in the iBook a snap. Be sure you are grounded before you perform a memory upgrade as any damage caused by static electricity will not be covered by the Apple Limited Product Warranty (touch a metal surface after you remove the keyboard).

Depending on which model iBook you have, it comes with either 32 megabytes or 64 megabytes of SDRAM, preinstalled on the iBook logic board. The memory expansion will accept a 32, 64, or 96MB DIMM, up to a 128 megabyte SO-DIMM, giving a maximum of 160 MB of memory on the earlier iBooks. The new iBooks, introduced in 2000, accept up to 256MB for a total of 320MB of RAM.

The memory must be a 144 pin, 1.25 inch (31mm) SDRAM SO-DIMM.

Place the iBook on a towel or other soft material before you upgrade.

STEP ONE
Release the two latches on both sides of the upper part of the keyboard.

Pull the latches down towards keys.

STEP TWO

Lift the keyboard up and place it face down on the iBook, and out of the way.

If there is an AirPort card already installed, it must be removed first.

STEP THREE

Remove the two screws that hold in the RAM shield.

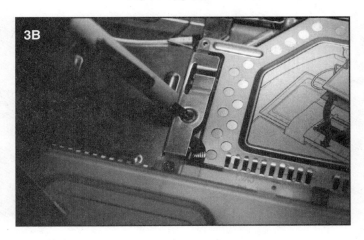

STEP FOUR
Remove the RAM shield

Move the AirPort antenna out of the way.

STEP FIVE
Insert the new RAM card into slot making sure it
lines up.

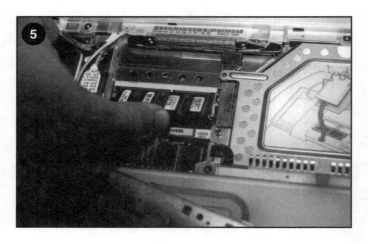

STEP SIX
Press it down so that it snaps into place.

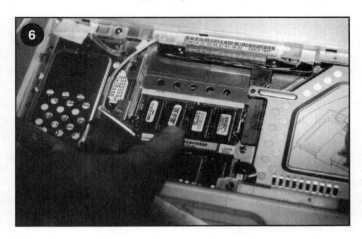

STEP SEVEN
Replace RAM shield making sure the AirPort antenna is out of the way.

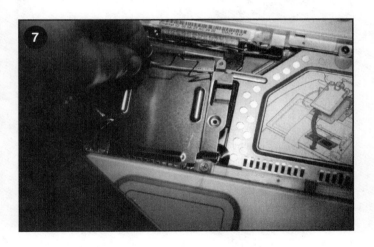

STEP EIGHT
Reinsert the two screws into the RAM shield.

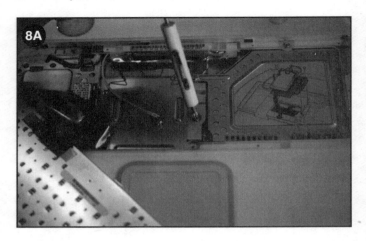

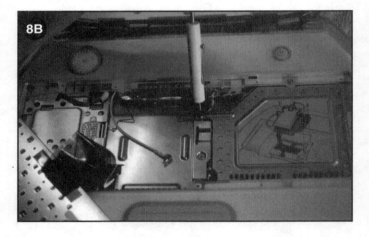

STEP NINE

Reinstall the keyboard. Be sure the tabs go into the bottom of the iBook first, then press gently onto the top of the keyboard so it snaps back in. Push the latches up to lock.

STEP TEN

Turn the iBook on and choose "About This Computer" from the Apple menu to ensure the memory is recognized.

PowerBook G3 Memory Upgrades

You use the same memory modules on the PowerBook G3 Series (Bronze keyboard) as the PowerBook G3 Series and the iMac, with a maximum of 384 MB. Since there are two available slots for memory upgrades, you need to check and see which configuration you have.

The 128 MB configuration may have a single 128 MB module or two-64 MB modules. You do not have to open the PowerBook to find out. Use Apple's System Profiler, located under the Apple Menu, and click the System Profile tab (should be default). Under "Memory Overview," click on the Built-in memory arrow. It will list how the Bottom and Top memory banks are configured.

Be sure you are grounded before you perform a memory upgrade as any damage caused by static electricity will not be covered by the Apple Limited Product Warranty.

STEP ONE

Place the PowerBook on a towel or other software material. Remove the AC power and the main battery.

STEP TWO

Remove the keyboard by releasing the screw behind the port access door on the back of the computer. Turn the screw several times counter-clockwise to release it. Apple says it does not ship the PowerBook with the keyboard locking screw engaged, so this step may or may not be needed prior to keyboard removal. The screw will not come out of the PowerBook.

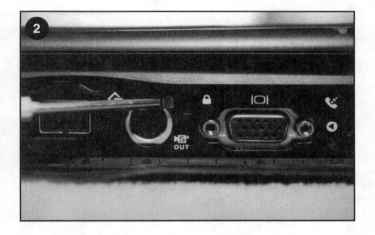

STEP THREE

Slide the two release latches (push them down) along the function key row towards the keys to release the keyboard.

STEP FOUR

Carefully lift and place the keyboard in front of you upside down and rest it over the trackpad.

STEP FIVE

Remove the three screws holding the heatsink to the processor.

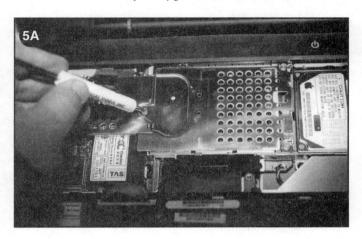

Apple says to use caution when lifting the heatsink since there may be material on the processor and it may stick to the heatsink.

Lift the front edge of the heatsink first, then remove it completely from the computer. Use the small handle to lift it up and out.

STEP SIX

Install the memory card. Be sure the card is positioned correctly. Start at an angle and insert so it is snug, then push the memory card in and down slightly until it snaps into position.

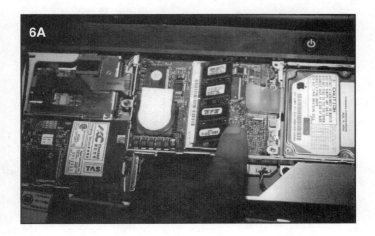

STEP SEVEN

Reinstall the heatsink, being careful not to damage the clip holding the RAM card to the processor card.

Check the ferrite bead on the display cable and make sure it is not under the heatsink. This could cause bending in the keyboard.

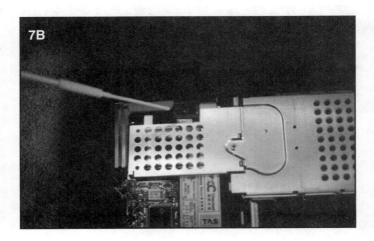

Before you screw the heatsink down, nudge the ferrite bead out of the way. Tighten all three screws back into the heatsink.

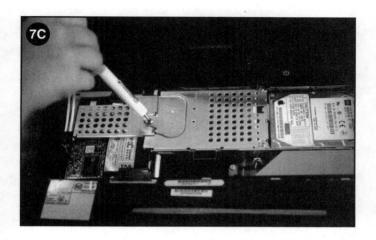

STEP EIGHT

Reinstall the keyboard by aligning the tabs on the bottom edge and making sure they fit before you press the keyboard into place.

STEP NINE

Slide the release latches back up to secure keyboard in place.

STEP TEN

Retighten the keyboard locking screw.

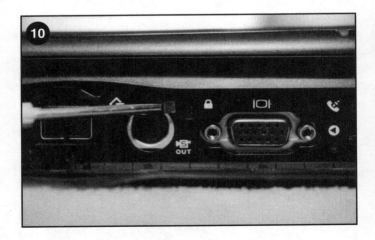

Step Eleven

Reinsert battery, AC power cable, and boot up Powerbook. Choose "About This Computer" from the Apple menu to ensure the memory is recognized.

G3 All-In-One Memory Upgrade

Since the Apple G3 All-In-One model was designed specifically for the education market, it is not featured here for memory upgrades. Educators should have their computer departments perform the upgrades.

RAM is expandable to 384 MB using three DIMM slots. Memory is 64-bit wide, 168-pin JEDEC-standard 3.3 V unbuffered SDRAM DIMMs.

G3 Basic Troubleshooting Guide

Many problems associated with the performance of your G3 Mac can be traced to minor problems like PCI cards or cables not seated properly (especially if you move your computer around), software glitches and incompatibilities, or bad RAM DIMMs, but sometimes there is a hardware component failure. When you consider the millions of items that are being manufactured each day, it is not uncommon for something to fail once in a while. If you are the unlucky person, there are steps that you can perform yourself to alleviate the problem before you have to take the G3 into a repair shop.

This troubleshooting guide will help you track down any problems you may have on your G3 model computer. It will provide a series of possible causes and several things you can do to try to fix the problem. Use this guide before you bring the G3 into your Apple Certified Technician. Often, you can fix the problem yourself simply by reseating a loose component, cable, or reinstalling software.

The information condensed in this guide comes from Apple's technical Web site and publications, technical notes, other Web tech sites, and the experience of Ken Ackley, a certified Apple technician who has fixed many a Macintosh. Remember that you may void your Apple warranty if you perform some of these fixes, so it is up to you to decide.

There are a few items I suggest you leave to the repair department. I don't fool around with the CRT (monitor) or power supply. Always make sure you are properly grounded. One small spark can ruin your entire computer. For added security buy yourself an AppleCare extended warranty. You invested hard-earned cash to buy your Mac. Invest in keeping it sound and working perfectly. AppleCare warranties are not expensive.

Often when simple troubleshooting does not do the job, a major part of the computer needs to be replaced. This could be the logic board, ROM DIMM, power supply, or CRT. Since you cannot purchase many of these items on your own, it is wise to have AppleCare for those rare times.

G3 Desktop Models

NOTE: Be sure you are properly grounded.

Apple Systems startup problems

Trouble

Fan on power supply is running.

No startup chime.

Screen is black.

Drive is not accessed at startup.

No LED on front of system.

Probable cause

Bad voltage regulator.

Voltage set for wrong geographic area.

Jumper block not set correctly for the power supply installed or processor module.

Possible fix

Inspect jumper block configuration at J28. Setting should be: 300 MHz is black, 350 MHz is blue, and 400 MHz is white. If the configuration is not correct, do not change it yourself since this will void Apple's warranty. Bring it to an Apple Certified Technician.

Check jumper block configuration at J16. Correct color for processor type installed is: red jumper (233 MHz), white jumper (266 MHz), or black jumper (300 MHz) and be sure jumper is facing the right direction.

Reseat voltage regulator.

Reseat processor module (locking arm in down position).

If nothing works, Apple recommends reseating the ROM DIMM, or replacing the voltage regulator, logic board, or processor module.

Trouble

Fan is running.

LED is on.

Drive is accessed at startup.

No startup chime.

Screen is black.

Probable cause

ROM DIMM is not seated properly.

Possible fix

Reseat ROM DIMM.

Trouble

No power.

Fan is not running.

No LED.

Probable cause

Power cord faulty or not secured at both ends.

Bad power outlet.

ADB cable not connected or bad.

Internal power cables not attached or bad.

Power supply setting wrong for your area.

Possible fix

Try another power cord (or reseat existing one), or outlet.

Reseat the voltage regulator.

Try another ADB cable or reseat the existing one.

Inspect internal power cables, reseat, or replace.

Inspect jumper block configuration at J28. Setting should be: 300 MHz is black, 350 MHz is blue, and 400 MHz is white. If it is not correct, do not change it yourself since this will void Apple's warranty. Bring it to an Apple Certified Technician.

If nothing works, Apple recommends resetting the Cuda chip, or logic board, or replacing the logic board.

Trouble

Computer begins to power up.

Fan and hard drive are spinning.

Power LED is lit.

No video.

Boot chime is followed by sound of breaking glass.

Probable cause

DRAM DIMMs or DOM DIMM not seated properly.

Bad DIMMs.

External or internal SCSI cable not secure.

Bad SCSI devices.

Possible fix

Reseat ROM DIMM or DRAM DIMMs.

Replace defective DIMMs (try removing and testing one at a time).

Reseat or replace SCSI cables.

Verify external SCSI devices are working.

Trouble

Clicking, chirping, thumping, or rubbing sound.

Probable cause

PCI cards not seated properly.

Bad hard drive or floppy drive.

Bad floppy drive cable.

Possible fix

Reseat all PCI cards.

Reseat or replace floppy drive cable.

Replace floppy drive (try another good one first).

Test hard drive, replace if bad.

If nothing works, Apple recommends replacing the
power supply, processor module, logic board, or I/O
card.

Trouble

System shuts down intermittently.

Probable cause

Air flow restricted around computer.

Power cord not firmly connected.

Internal battery needs replacing.

Possible fix

Be sure ventilation around the computer is unrestricted. If the thermal protection circuit shut down the computer, wait at least half an hour before restarting

Reseat or replace power cord.

Replace battery.

If noting works, Apple recommends resetting the Cuda chip, or logic board, or replacing the power supply, logic board, or processor module.

Trouble

System intermittently crashes or hangs.

Probable cause

System software corrupt.

Extension conflict.

Application software being used is not compatible with computer or system version.

DIMMs not seated properly.

Possible fix

Use the latest system software and compatible application software for your computer.

Restart with extensions off. Use the minimum extensions to see if symptoms persist. If you recently installed new software, check it first to see if it installed a conflicting extension.

Zap PRAM. Hold down **Command-Option-P-R** keys until you hear the startup sounds twice, or use TechTool.

Reseat or replace defective DIMMs.

If nothing works, Apple recommends replacing the logic board or processor module.

Trouble

During startup, you see the following message: "This startup disk will not work on this Macintosh model."

Probable cause

Corrupted system software on hard drive.

Startup disk is bad.

Possible fix

Try another startup disk.

Perform a clean install of system software.

Be sure you are using the correct version of system software and enabler 770 is present.

Trouble

Error chords.

One-part error chord (sound of breaking glass) sounds during startup sequence.

Probable cause

Bad hard drive.

Bad floppy drive.

Possible fix

Reseat IDE data cable from hard drive.

Reseat floppy drive cable.

Replace hard or floppy drive (test with a different one first).

Reseat the processor module.

If nothing works Apple recommends replacing the logic board or processor module.

Audio (speaker) problems

Trouble

No sound from speaker.

Probable cause

Volume setting not correct (or mute is selected).

Microphone or external speakers connected.

Sound cable is not seated properly in logic board.

Bad speaker.

Possible fix

Adjust volume settings in control panel.

Disconnect microphone or external speakers and test.

Zap PRAM. Hold down **Command-Option-P-R** keys during startup or use TechTool.

Reseat cable from speaker into logic board.

Insert headphones or external speakers into the external jack.

If sound comes from the external jack, replace the internal speaker or logic board.

If the external jack does not emit sound, Apple recommends replacing the I/O audio card or logic board.

Floppy drive problems

Trouble

Internal floppy drive does not operate.

Probable cause

Bad disk in drive.

Floppy drive cable not seated or bad.

Bad floppy drive.

Possible fix

Try another floppy disk.

Reseat or replace floppy drive cable.

Replace floppy drive.

If nothing works, Apple recommends replacing the logic board or processor module.

Trouble

During system startup a floppy disk ejects from floppy drive and the monitor displays an icon with blinking "X".

Probable cause

Bad startup disk.

Bad floppy drive or cable.

Possible fix

Try another system disk.

Reseat or replace floppy drive cable.

Replace floppy drive.

If nothing works, Apple recommends replacing the logic board or processor module.

Trouble

Disk does not eject from floppy drive.

Probable cause

Bad disk, shutter stuck.

Floppy drive cable not seated or bad.

Bad floppy drive.

Possible fix

Eject disk manually by carefully inserting opened paper clip into hole near floppy drive slot.

Use keyboard shortcut **Cloverleaf-E**.

Use keyboard shortcut **Cloverleaf-Shift-1**.

Switch off computer. Hold down mouse button while you switch computer on.

Replace floppy drive cable or drive.

If nothing works, Apple recommends replacing the logic board or processor module.

Trouble

Floppy drive tries to eject disk, but disk does not come out.

Probable cause

Floppy drive bezel slots not aligned correctly.

Stuck floppy disk.

Bad floppy drive.

Possible fix

Reseat floppy drive bezel and drive to realign slots.

Manually remove disk.

Replace floppy drive.

Trouble

Internal floppy drive runs continuously.

Probable cause

Bad floppy disk.

Bad floppy drive or cable.

Possible fix

Try another disk. If problem persists replace floppy drive cable or drive.

If nothing works, Apple recommends replacing the logic board or processor module.

Trouble

MS-DOS drive does not recognize a disk formatted on a 1.4 MB drive.

Probable cause

Floppy disks not formatted on MS-DOS drive.

Possible fix

Format all disks on the MS-DOS drive first.

Hard drive problems

Trouble

Single internal hard drive does not operate (drive isn't spinning).

Probable cause

Bad hard drive power cable.

Bad hard drive.

Possible fix

Reseat or replace hard drive power cable.

Replace hard drive.

If nothing works, Apple recommends replacing the power supply.

Trouble

No internal SCSI drives are operating.

Probable cause

SCSI ID conflict.

Termination is wrong on the SCSI chain.

Bad drives.

Possible fix

Inspect and insure that all devices have unique SCSI ID number.

Disconnect any external SCSI devices and see if they are terminated properly (only last device in SCSI chain should be terminated).

Reseat or replace internal SCSI data cable connected to the device not working.

If nothing works, Apple recommends replacing the power supply, logic board, or processor module.

Trouble

Computer works with internal or external SCSI devices but not with both.

Probable cause

SCSI ID conflict.

Termination of SCSI chain not correct.

Possible fix

Ensure that all SCSI devices have a unique SCSI ID number.

Check terminator on external device and replace if necessary.

Ensure that only the last SCSI device on the chain is terminated.

Network problems (Ethernet)

Trouble

Ethernet connection drops off line by itself.

Probable cause

Incorrect Ethernet driver.

Possible fix

Install Ethernet driver 2.0.4 or later.

Peripheral problems

Cursor or mouse problems

Trouble

Cursor on screen does not move.

Probable cause

Dirty mouse.

ADB connection is loose or cable is bad on computer ADB port or keyboard.

Possible fix

Clean mouse.

Reseat ADB connection.

Connect mouse to different ADB port instead. If mouse works, replace keyboard.

Reseat or replace ADB cable.

Replace mouse if it does not work on any ADB port.

If nothing works, Apple recommends replacing the logic board or processor module.

Trouble

Cursor moves on screen, but clicking mouse button has no effect.

Probable cause

Bad mouse.

Software conflict.

Possible fix

Restart computer from floppy or bootable CD.

Reinstall system software.

Replace mouse.

If nothing works, Apple recommends replacing the logic board.

Trouble

Double-clicking the mouse doesn't open application, disk, or server.

Probable cause

There is more than one system folders on your hard drive.

Software conflict.

ADB connection is faulty.

Possible fix

Remove duplicate system folders if they exist.

Zap PRAM. Hold down **Command-Option-P-R** keys during startup or use TechTool.

Connect mouse to different ADB port if on keyboard. If it works, then replace the keyboard.

Replace ADB cable.

Clean mouse.

If mouse fails on all ADB port connections, replace the mouse.

If nothing works, Apple recommends replacing the logic board.

Keyboard problems

Trouble

No response at all to any key on keyboard.

Probable cause

ADB connection is loose or faulty.

Bad keyboard or cable.

Possible fix

Reseat ADB connection.

Replace ADB keyboard cable.

Replace keyboard.

If nothing works, Apple recommends replacing the logic board.

Printer problems

Trouble

Serial printer does not work.

Probable cause

Printer drivers corrupted or not installed.

Printer not selected in Chooser.

System software corrupted.

Printer cable bad or not seated properly.

Possible fix

Reinstall printer drivers.

Perform clean install of system software.

Be sure that system software and printer driver versions are compatible (check with printer vendor).

Reseat or replace printer interface cable.

If nothing works, Apple recommends replacing the logic board.

Trouble

Network printer does not print.

Probable cause

Network connection is broken.

Printer drivers corrupted or not installed.

Printer not selected in Chooser.

System software corrupted.

Possible fix

Inspect network connections and correct if broken.

Select printer in Chooser.

Reinstall printer drivers, or clean install system software.

Ensure printer driver and system software are compatible (check printer vendor).

If nothing works, Apple recommends replacing the logic board.

Trouble

Color StyleWriter 4500 printer does not work.

Probable cause

Corrupted or outdated printer driver.

Possible fix

Install Color StyleWriter 4500 driver, version 1.1 or later which you can obtain from Apple's Web site at **http://www.apple.com/support/**.

CD-ROM problems

Trouble

CD-ROM drive does not work.

Probable cause

Bad disk.

CD-ROM drivers corrupted or not installed.

CD-ROM data cable not seated properly or bad.

Bad CD-ROM drive.

Possible fix

Try another disk.

Reinstall CD-ROM drivers.

Reseat CD-ROM data cable at logic board connector as well as at CD-ROM connector.

Replace CD-ROM data cable.

Replace CDROM drive.

Trouble

Macintosh does not display CD-ROM icon once CD is inserted in drive.

Probable cause

Bad disk.

CD-ROM drivers corrupted or not installed.

CD-ROM data cable not seated properly or bad.

Possible fix

Try another disk.

Reinstall CD-ROM drivers.

Reseat CD-ROM data cable at logic board connector as well as at CD-ROM connector.

Replace CD-ROM data cable.

Replace CD-ROM drive.

Trouble

CD-ROM drive does not eject disks.

Probable cause

CD-ROM drive not installed properly.

Disk not inserted all the way.

Possible fix

Apple recommends that new poron bumpers (part number 922-3554) on the back of the CD-ROM carrier, where the carrier makes contact with the metal tabs on the chassis, be replaced.

Trouble

CD-ROM drive ejects at startup time.

Probable cause

CD-ROM not installed correctly.

Possible fix

Apple recommends that the CD-ROM drive carrier be mounted forward and the drive mounted as far back as possible, so there is space between the bezel button and CD-ROM button.

Trouble

CD-ROM drive vibrates and is unusually loud when CD spins.

Probable cause

Vibration hitting chassis.

Possible fix

Apple recommends that a rubber bumper (part number 922-3678) be installed on the right side of the CD-ROM drive between the two screws.

Video/monitor problems

Trouble

Screen is black.

Boot tone heard.

Drive boots up.

Fan is running.

LED is on.

Probable cause

Monitor's brightness control not correct.

Monitor cable not seated properly or defective.

DIMMs bad or not seated correctly.

Bad monitor.

Possible fix

Use brightness control and adjust.

Zap PRAM. Hold down **Command-Option-P-R** keys or use TechTool.

Replace monitor cable.

Reseat or replace DIMMs.

Replace bad monitor (try another one first).

If nothing works, Apple recommends resetting the Cuda chip or logic board or replacing the logic board, or processor module.

Trouble

Screen is black.

No boot tone.

Drive not working

Fan is running.

LED is lit.

Probable cause

DIMMs bad or not seated properly.

Possible fix

Reseat or replace DIMMs (test one at a time).

If this does not work, Apple recommends resetting the Cuda chip or logic board, or replacing the logic board, power supply, or processor module.

Trouble

Boot tone is heard.

Screen lights up.

Nothing shows up on screen.

Probable cause

Bad monitor cable or monitor.

Possible fix

Reseat or replace monitor cable.

Try another monitor.

Replace defective monitor.

If nothing works, Apple recommends resetting the Cuda chip or logic board.

Trouble

Screen is black.

No boot tone heard.

Drive not operating.

Fan is running.

LED is lit.

Probable cause

DIMMs not seated properly or defective.

Possible fix

Reseat or replace defective DIMMs.

If this doesn't work, Apple recommends resetting the Cuda chip or logic board, or replacing the logic board, power supply, or processor module.

Trouble

Boot tone is heard.

Screen lights up.

Nothing appears on the screen.

Probable cause

Monitor cable is bad or not seated properly.

Bad monitor.

Possible fix

Reseat or replace monitor cable.

Try another monitor.

Replace monitor.

If nothing works, Apple recommends resetting the Cuda chip or logic board, or replacing logic board or processor module.

Trouble

Horizontal flickering lines when viewing the monitor.

Probable cause

Apple Video Play application with video mirroring on.

Possible fix

Apple recommends replacing the Audio/Video card with a Version II Audio/Video card (p/n 661-2044).

G3 All-In-One Model

Apple Systems startup problems

Trouble

Fan is running.

No startup chime.

Screen is black.

Drive not accessed at startup.

No LED on front of system.

Probable cause

Voltage regulator not correct.

ROM DIMM not seated properly.

Jumpers for processor not correct.

Processor module not seated correctly.

Possible fix

Check to see that jumper block configuration at J28 is correct. 300 MHz is black, 350 MHz is blue, and 400 MHz is white. If it is not correct, do not change it yourself since this will void Apple's warranty. Bring it to an Apple Certified Technician.

Check jumper block configuration at J16. Make sure jumper block is correct color for processor type installed—red jumper (233 MHz), white jumper (266 MHz), or black jumper (300 MHz)) and faces in the right direction.

Reseat the ROM DIMM or processor module (locking arm down).

If nothing works, Apple recommends replacing the voltage regulator, logic board, processor module, or analog board.

Trouble

Fan is running.

LED is on.

Drive operational at startup.

No startup chime.

Screen is black.

Probable cause

Voltage regulator not correct.

ROM DIMM not seated properly.

Possible fix

Check to see jumper block configuration at J28 is correct. 300 MHz is black, 350 MHz is blue, and 400 MHz is white. If it is not correct, do not change it yourself since they will void Apple's warranty. Bring it to an Apple Certified Technician.

Reseat ROM DIMM.

Trouble

No power.

Fan not running.

No LED.

Probable cause

Power cord not seated firmly.

ROM DIMM not seated properly.

Internal power cables not secured firmly.

Possible fix

Try a different power cord or reseat existing one, and internal power cables.

Reseat ROM DIMM.

Reseat processor module.

Check to see jumper block configuration at J28 is correct. 300 MHz is black, 350 MHz is blue, and 400 MHz is white. If it is not correct, do not change it yourself since this will void Apple's warranty. Bring it to an Apple Certified Technician.

If nothing works, Apple recommends resetting the Cuda chip or logic board.

Trouble

Fan is running.

LED is on.

Drive is operational at startup.

No startup chime.

Screen is black.

Probable cause

Voltage regulator not set correctly.

ROM DIMM not seated properly.

Possible fix

Check to see jumper block configuration at J28 is correct. 300 MHz is black, 350 MHz is blue, and 400 MHz is white. If it is not correct, do not change it yourself since this will void Apple's warranty. Bring it to an Apple Certified Technician.

Reseat ROM DIMM.

Trouble

No power.

Fan not running.

No LED.

Probable cause

External power cord or internal power cables defective, or not secured firmly.

ROM DIMM not seated firmly.

Processor module not seated firmly.

Possible fix

Reseat or replace power cord or internal cables. Try another cord.

Reseat ROM DIMM.

Reseat the processor module.

Check to see jumper block configuration at J28 is correct. 300 MHz is black, 350 MHz is blue, and 400 MHz is white. If it is not correct, do not change it yourself since this will void Apple's warranty. Bring it to an Apple Certified Technician.

Check jumper block configuration at J16. Make sure jumper block is correct color for processor type installed—red jumper (233 MHz), white jumper (266 MHz), or a black jumper (300 MHz) and faces in the right direction.

If nothing works, Apple recommends resetting the Cuda chip, or logic board, or replacing the voltage regulator, power supply, analog board, logic board, or processor module.

Trouble

Clicking, chirping, thumping, or rubbing sound.

Probable cause

PCI card not seated properly or defective.

Bad hard drive or cable.

Bad floppy drive or cable.

Possible fix

Reseat all PCI cards. Replace defective one.

Replace defective hard drive or cable (test with another good one first).

Replace floppy drive or cable (test with another good one first).

If nothing works, Apple recommends replacing the power supply, analog board, processor module, logic board, or I/O card.

Trouble

System shuts down intermittently.

Probable cause

Ventilation ports clogged or blocked.

Power cord not seated firmly.

Internal battery weak.

Possible fix

Ensure that there is ample air flow around the computer.

Reseat the power cord or try another.

Check battery level.

If nothing works, Apple recommends resetting the Cuda chip or logic board, or replacing the power supply, logic board, or processor module.

Trouble

System intermittently crashes or freezes.

Probable cause

System software corrupted.

Application software not compatible with system.

SDRAM DIMMs not seated properly or bad.

Possible fix

Reinstall system software.

Ensure that application software is Power Mac compatible.

Restart with extensions off, look for extension conflict (start with new application software if just installed). Turn off bad INIT.

Zap PRAM. Hold down **Command-Option-P-R** keys or use TechTool.

Reseat all SDRAM DIMMs, or replace defective ones (test one at a time).

If nothing works, Apple recommends replacing the logic board or processor module.

Trouble

During startup, following message is displayed on monitor: "This startup disk will not work on this Macintosh model."

Probable cause

Bad startup disk.

System software corrupted or wrong version for that model.

Possible fix

Try another startup disk.

Do a clean install of system software.

Trouble

Computer boots to the desktop.

Only white menu bar appears.

No icons appear.

Mouse freezes.

Probable cause

Front panel control board cable not connected or bad.

Possible fix

Inspect the cable connected to the P4 connector on the front panel control board and reseat.

If nothing works, Apple recommends replacing the front panel control board.

Error chords

Trouble

One-part error chord sounds audible during startup sequence.

Probable cause

Defective hard drive.

Defective floppy drive.

Processor module not seated firmly.

Possible fix

Replace hard drive.

Replace floppy drive.

Reseat processor module.

If nothing works, Apple recommends replacing the logic board or processor module.

Trouble

An eight-part error chord (death chimes) audible during startup sequence.

Probable cause

Bad DIMMs or not DIMMs seated correctly.

Possible fix

Reseat or replace DIMMs.

If nothing works, Apple recommends replacing logic board.

Audio (speaker) problems

Trouble

No sound from speaker.

Probable cause

Volume settings not correct.

Bad speaker.

Speaker not connected to logic board.

Possible fix

Check volume controls in sound control panel (mute not checked).

Zap PRAM. Hold down **Command-Option-P-R** keys during startup or use TechTool.

Disconnect any microphones or external speakers.

Verify speaker is plugged into logic board.

Plug headphones or external speakers into the external jack.

If the external jack works, replace the internal speaker or logic board.

If the external jack doesn't work, replace I/O Audio card, speaker, or logic board.

Floppy drive problems

Trouble

Floppy drive internal floppy drive does not operate.

Probable cause

Bad floppy drive or cable.

Bad or defective disk.

Possible fix

Try another disk.

Replace floppy drive or cable.

If nothing works, Apple recommends replacing the logic board or processor module.

Trouble

During system startup, a disk ejects and display shows icon with blinking "X".

Probable cause

Bad system disk.

Bad floppy drive or cable.

Possible fix

Try another good system disk.

Replace floppy drive or cable.

If nothing works, Apple recommends replacing the logic board or processor module.

Trouble

Disk does not eject from floppy drive.

Probable cause

Disk stuck, bad shutter.

Bad floppy drive or cable.

Possible fix

Use shortcut **Cloverleaf-E** on keyboard.

Use shortcut **Cloverleaf-Shift-1** on keyboard.

Eject disk manually by carefully inserting opened paper clip into hole near floppy drive slot.

Reboot computer and hold down mouse button as computer starts up.

Replace floppy drive or cable.

If nothing works, Apple recommends replacing the logic board or processor module.

Trouble
  Drive attempts to eject disk, but doesn't succeed.

  Probable cause
   Disk stuck, bad shutter.

   Bad floppy drive or cable.

   Floppy drive bezel not aligned.

  Possible fix
   Reseat floppy drive bezel and the floppy drive so bezel slot aligns correctly with drive.

   Eject disk manually by carefully inserting opened paper clip into hole near floppy drive slot.

   Replace floppy drive.

Trouble
  Internal floppy drive runs continuously.

  Probable cause
   Bad disk.

   Bad floppy drive or cable.

  Possible fix
   Try another disk.

   Replace floppy drive or cable

   If nothing works, Apple recommends replacing the logic board or processor module.

Trouble
  MS-DOS drive does not recognize a disk formatted on a 1.4 MB drive.

Probable cause

Disks not formatted on MS-DOS drive first.

Possible fix

Format all disks with MS-DOS drive first.

Hard drive problems

Trouble

Single internal hard drive does not operate and drive doesn't spin.

Probable cause

Bad hard drive or power cable.

Possible fix

Replace hard drive or cable.

If nothing works Apple recommends replacing the power supply.

Trouble

No internal SCSI drives operate.

Probable cause

SCSI ID conflict.

Bad SCSI device on chain.

SCSI devices not properly terminated.

Bad SCSI data cable.

Possible fix

Verify that each SCSI device has unique ID number.

Verify each SCSI device is working.

Check internal SCSI devices for proper termination.

Reseat or replace internal SCSI data cable.

If nothing works, Apple recommends replacing the power supply, logic board, or processor module.

Trouble
Works with internal or external SCSI devices but not with both.

Probable cause
SCSI ID conflict.

Terminator on external device needs replacing.

Terminator on internal SCSI data cable is not terminated.

Possible fix
Verify that each device has unique SCSI ID number.

Replace terminators.

Network problems

Trouble
Ethernet connection drops off line by itself.

Probable cause
Bad Ethernet drivers.

Network connection faulty.

Possible fix
Install Ethernet driver 2.0.4 or later.

Check network connection for break.

Peripheral problems

Cursor or mouse problems

Trouble
Cursor does not move when you are using mouse.

Probable cause

Dirty mouse.

Keyboard ADB port not functioning.

ADB cable bad or not seated properly.

Possible fix

Clean mouse.

Make sure mouse connection is firm.

Connect mouse to ADB port on computer instead of keyboard. If works, replace keyboard.

Reseat or replace ADB cable.

Replace mouse.

If nothing works, Apple recommends replacing the logic board or processor module.

Trouble

Cursor moves, but clicking mouse button has no effect.

Probable cause

Bad or dirty mouse.

Possible fix

Restart computer from floppy or CD that has system on it.

Clean mouse.

Replace mouse.

If nothing works, Apple recommends replacing the logic board.

Trouble

Double-clicking mouse doesn't open application, disk, or server.

Probable cause

Software conflict; you may have more than one system folder on hard drive.

Bad mouse or ADB connection.

Possible fix

Remove second system folder if one exists.

Zap PRAM. Hold down **Command-Option-P-R** keys during startup or use TechTool.

Connect mouse to computer's ADB port if it is connected to keyboard. If it works, replace the keyboard.

Replace mouse if it doesn't work on any ADB port.

If nothing works, Apple recommends replacing the logic board

Keyboard problems

Trouble

No response to any key on keyboard.

Probable cause

Bad keyboard.

Bad keyboard cable.

ADB connection not firm.

Possible fix

Reseat ADB port connections.

Replace keyboard cable.

Replace keyboard.

If nothing works, Apple recommends replacing the logic board.

Printer problems

Trouble

Serial printer does not work.

Probable cause

Printer drivers are incorrect version or are not installed.

Printer not selected in Chooser.

Printer cables not seated properly or defective.

Possible fix

Reinstall printer drivers, or perform clean install of system software.

Select printer in Chooser.

Reseat or replace printer cable.

If nothing works, Apple recommends replacing the logic board.

Trouble

Network printer does not print.

Probable cause

Network connection broken.

Printer drivers are incorrect version or not installed.

Printer not selected in Chooser.

Printer cables not seated properly or defective.

Possible fix

Reinstall network or printer software.

Perform clean install of system software.

Check network connection for breaks.

Select printer in Chooser.

Ensure that system software version used is correct.

If nothing works, Apple recommends replacing the logic board.

CD-ROM problems

Trouble
CD-ROM drive does not work.

Probable cause
Bad CD-ROM drive or disk.

Bad cable.

Possible fix
Try another disk.

Replace CD-ROM drive.

Reseat or replace CD-ROM power or SCSI cable.

Trouble
Macintosh does not display CD-ROM icon once CD is inserted in drive.

Probable cause
Bad or not installed CD-ROM drivers.

No disk in CD-ROM drive.

Cable not seated correctly.

Possible fix
Try another disk.

Reinstall CD-ROM drivers and insure they are compatible with system software being used.

Reseat CD-ROM data cable at logic board connector and at CD-ROM connector.

Replace CD-ROM drive mechanism or data cable.

Video/monitor problems

Trouble

Screen is black or green.

Boot tone is heard.

Drive operates.

Fan is on and running.

LED is lit.

Probable cause

Brightness control not set correctly.

A/V I/O card not seated correctly or bad.

Cable connections on CRT video or analog board loose, not seated, or bad.

Possible fix

Adjust brightness on monitor.

Zap RAM. Hold down **Command-Option-P-R** keys during startup or use TechTool.

Reseat or replace the Audio/Video I/O card.

Reseat or replace cable connections on analog and CRT video board.

Verify that wires P505 connect to P913 and P905 on the power supply board, and that P507 connects to P908 on the power supply.

Reseat or replace RGB monitor cable.

Reseat or replace all SDRAM DIMMs (test one at a time).

If nothing works, Apple recommends resetting the Cuda chip or logic board, or replacing the logic board or processor module.

Trouble

Screen is black or green.

No boot tone.

Drive does not operate.

Fan is running.

LED is lit.

Probable cause

DIMMs not seated or bad.

A/V I/O card not seated or bad.

Cable connections on CRT video or analog board not seated or bad.

Bad RGB cable.

Possible fix

Reseat or replace DIMMs.

Reseat cables on analog and CRT video board or replace. Check that wires P505 connect to P913 and P905 on the power supply board, and that P507 connects to P908 on the power supply.

Reseat or replace RGB monitor cable.

If nothing works, Apple recommends resetting the Cuda chip or logic board, or replacing the analog board, power supply, or processor module.

Trouble

Boot tone is heard.

Screen lights up.

Nothing is seen on screen.

Probable cause

A/V I/O card not seated properly.

Cables not seated properly on analog board or power supply

Possible fix

Reseat or replace all cables on the analog and video boards and power supply.

Reseat or replace, if defective, the Audio/Video I/O card.

Inspect and insure that the wires P505 from the analog board connect to P913 and P905 on the power supply board, and that P507 on the analog board connects to P908 on the power supply.

If nothing works, Apple recommends resetting the Cuda Chip or logic board, or replacing the analog board, logic board, or processor module.

Trouble
    Predominant color tint appears on monitor.

  Probable cause
    Video adjustments off.

    Cable connection on analog or video board loose or not seated properly.

    RGB cable not seated or defective.

    Bad monitor.

  Possible fix
    Adjust video.

    Reseat RGB video cable or replace if defective.

    Reseat cable on analog or video boards or replace if defective.

    If nothing works, Apple recommends replacing the analog/video board or CRT.

Trouble
    Horizontal flickering lines when viewing Apple Video Play application with video mirroring on.

  Probable cause
    Audio/video card.

Possible fix

Replace the Audio/Video card with a Version II Audio/Video card (p/n 661-2044).

G3 Blue and White Model

Apple Systems startup problems

Trouble

Fan on power supply is running.

No startup tone.

Screen is black.

Drive not operational at startup.

No LED on front of system.

Probable cause

Wrong voltage supply.

Jumper block configured wrong.

DIMMs not seated properly or bad.

Processor module not seated properly.

Possible fix

Reseat or replace the DIMMs.

Check to see that jumper block configuration at J25 is correct. 300 MHz is black, 350 MHz is blue, and 400 MHz is white. If it is not correct, do not change it yourself since this will void Apple's warranty. Bring it to an Apple Certified Technician.

Check the power supply and make sure the voltage switch is set correctly. It must be set manually. There are two switches that allow you to set a range from 100–130 volts or 220–270 volts.

Reseat the processor module and lock it into place.

If nothing works, Apple recommends resetting or replacing the logic board.

Trouble

Fan is running.

LED is on.

Drive is accessed at startup.

No startup chime.

Screen is black.

Probable cause

Cabling to monitor, speaker and or microphone ports not correct.

Wrong voltage.

Bad or not firmly seated DIMMs.

Possible fix

Check to see that jumper block configuration at J25 is correct. 300 MHz is black, 350 MHz is blue, and 400 MHz is white. If it is not correct, do not change it yourself since this will void Apple's warranty. Bring it to an Apple Certified Technician.

Reseat SDRAM DIMMs, or replace if defective (test one at a time).

Be sure cable connections to the monitor, speaker and microphone ports in the rear of the unit are correct and secure.

Trouble

Memory error dialog box message appears on the screen.

Probable cause

DIMMs not seated properly or defective.

Wrong DIMMs installed.

Possible fix

Reseat DIMMs.

Replace defective DIMMs (test one at a time).

Use only correct PC-100 SDRAM DIMMs.

Trouble

Computer begins to power up.

Fan is working.

Hard drive is spinning.

Power LED is lit.

No video.

Probable cause

DIMMs not seated properly or defective.

Wrong voltage.

Processor card not seated properly.

Internal SCSI cabling not secure.

Installed cards not seated properly.

Possible fix

Reseat DIMMs.

Replace defective DIMMs (test one at a time).

Check to see that jumper block configuration at J25 is correct. 300 MHz is black, 350 MHz is blue, and 400 MHz is white. If it is not correct, do not change it yourself since this will void Apple's warranty. Bring it to an Apple Certified Technician.

Reseat the processor card, other cards, and reseat all cables.

Remove all cards, except video card, and disconnect hard drives from the logic board. If you have video, video card is fine.

If nothing works, Apple recommends replacing the video card, logic board, or processor.

Trouble

Clicking, chirping, thumping, or rubbing sound.

Probable cause

Installed card in slot not working.

CD-ROM or Zip drive carrier not seated properly.

Bad hard drive.

Possible fix

Remove all PCI cards one at a time and test.

Reseat the CD-ROM or Zip drive carrier and cables.

Replace hard drive or Zip drive.

If nothing works, Apple recommends replacing the power supply, processor module, logic board, or I/O card.

Trouble

System shuts down intermittently.

Probable cause

Fan not working properly.

Overheated heat sink.

Power plug not seated firmly.

Bad battery.

Possible fix

Ensure that the fan cable is connected and fan works.

Work with no obstructions to the air vents and make sure the access panel is closed to prevent the heat sink from overheating.

Reseat or replace the power cord.

Check battery. Replace if bad.

If nothing works, Apple recommends resetting the Cuda chip or logic board, or replacing the power supply, logic board, or processor module.

Trouble

System intermittently crashes or freezes.

Probable cause

Bad system software.

Bad application software, not Power Mac compatible.

Extension conflicts.

Bad memory.

Possible fix

Reseat DIMMs, or remove one at a time and test, or replace defective ones.

Verify you are using system software version 8.5.1 with Mac OS ROM 1.2.

Verify that the application software you are using is compatible.

Do a clean install of system software with the CD that came with the computer.

Reboot with extensions off (or remove the extension if you just installed a new software program that installed one).

Run Disk Aid or Norton Utilities.

Zap PRAM. Hold down **Command-Option-P-R** during startup or use TechTool.

If nothing works, Apple recommends resetting or replacing the logic board or replacing the processor module.

Trouble

During startup, the following message is displayed on your monitor: "This startup disk will not work on this Macintosh model."

Probable cause

Bad startup disk.

Wrong system software on disk.

Possible fix

Verify that the system software is version 8.5.1 or later with Mac OS ROM 1.2.

Perform a clean install of system software with the CD that came with the computer.

Trouble

System freezes during normal operation.

Probable cause

Bad USB devices attached.

Extension conflict.

Corrupted system software.

Possible fix

Turn off extensions using the Extension Manager in Controls Panels. Or boot with Extensions off by holding down the Shift key during startup.

Replace Extensions one at a time and booting up the system after each one to find the one causing the conflict. If you installed new third-party software, start with that first.

Use Conflict Catcher by Casady & Greene.

Perform a clean install of system software with the CD that came with your computer.

Disconnect all USB devices, reconnecting one at a time to see which is bad.

Start with mouse, keyboard, etc.

Reseat DIMMs or replace if defective (test one at a time first).

If nothing works, Apple recommends resetting or replacing the logic board or replacing the processor module.

Trouble

No power; system is deader than a doornail.

Probable cause

Bad power supply.

No power coming from outlet.

Bad power cord.

Bad LEDs on logic board.

Bad USB connection on keyboard.

Possible fix

If LEDs DS7 and DS8 on logic board are not both on or off, there is a problem.

Use a different power outlet.

Try another power cord.

Replace power supply.

Be sure voltage switch is correctly set; this is important if you bought your computer in another country and moved.

Disconnect keyboard and power up the computer using the reset button on front. Replace keyboard if that worked.

If nothing works, Apple recommends resetting the Cida chip or logic board, or replacing the logic board.

Trouble

Computer beeps once at startup.

Probable cause

No RAM is installed or detected.

Processor module not seated properly.

Possible fix

Reseat DIMMs.

Install PC-100 SDRAM DIMMs if none present.

Replace defective DIMMs (test one at a time first).

Reseat processor module.

If nothing works, Apple recommends replacing the processor module or logic board.

Trouble

Computer beeps twice at startup.

Probable cause

Incompatible RAM installed.

Processor module not seated properly.

Possible fix

Be sure only PC-100 SDRAM DIMMs are installed, not EDO memory.

Replace defective DIMMs (test one at a time first).

Reseat processor module.

If nothing works, Apple recommends replacing the processor module or logic board.

Trouble

Computer beeps three times at startup.

Probable cause

RAM banks failed memory testing.

Processor module not seated properly.

Possible fix

Replace the existing DIMMs one at a time with good PC-100 SDRAM DIMMs.

Reseat processor module.

If nothing works, Apple recommends replacing the processor module or logic board.

Trouble

Computer beeps four or five beeps at startup.

Probable cause

Bad ROM.

Possible fix

None. You must replace the logic board.

Audio (speaker) problems

Trouble

No sound from computer's speaker.

Probable cause

Volume settings not correct or in mute mode.

Software conflict.

Speaker cable not connected.

Possible fix

Reboot with extensions off.

Disconnect microphones or external speakers.

Check volume settings in control panel. Make sure Mute is not selected.

Zap PRAM. Hold down **Command-Option-P-R** during startup or use TechTool.

Check speaker cable (J34) and make sure it is plugged into logic board.

Plug headphones or external speakers into the external jack.

Replace the internal speaker if the external jack works. If it does not, replace the logic board.

Hard drive problems

Trouble

Single internal hard drive does not operate and doesn't spin.

Probable cause

Driver corrupt or not present.

Cable connections to hard drive faulty.

Power cable to hard drive defective.

Possible fix

Replace hard drive data cable or power cable.

If nothing works, Apple recommends replacing the hard drive, and reinstalling IDE device driver and system software, or replacing the power supply.

Trouble

No internal SCSI drives operate.

Probable cause

SCSI ID conflict.

SCSI PCI card not seated properly.

Possible fix

Reseat SCSI PCI card.

Ensure all SCSI devices have unique number.

Disconnect external SCSI devices and reconnect one by one to locate troubled unit.

If nothing works, Apple recommends replacing the SCSI PCI or power supply.

Trouble

Computer works with internal or external SCSI devices but not with both.

Probable cause

SCSI ID conflict.

SCSI termination wrong.

Bad or improperly seated SCSI card.

Bad SCSI drive cables.

Possible fix

Ensure that each device has unique SCSI ID.

Reseat SCSI cable to the SCSI card.

Replace terminator on external SCSI device.

Ensure that the SCSI device at end of internal SCSI data cable is the only device terminated.

Remove one SCSI device at a time to find bad one.

Reseat the SCSI card.

Replace SCSI drive cables one at a time.

Replace SCSI card.

Miscellaneous trouble

Trouble

Small pieces of metal found loose in computer, computer rattles.

Probable cause

You broke something.

Your dropped the computer.

Your two-year-old played daddy and inserted something into the floppy or Zip drive.

Possible fix

Extract any loose metal in the computer and inspect everything to see where metal came from.

Test computer to see if it still functions.

Don't drop it again.

Network problems

Trouble

Ethernet connection drops off line by itself.

Probable cause

Faulty cables.

Ethernet drivers corrupted.

Network connection faulty.

Possible fix

Try another Ethernet cable.

Reinstall the Ethernet driver.

Check the network for loose cables.

Trouble

Unable to switch to the Ethernet network option in the control panel.

Probable cause

Network or cable is not correct.

Extension conflicts.

Possible fix

Try a different Ethernet cable.

Check the network for breaks.

Zap PRAM. Hold down **Command-Option-P-R** during startup or use Techtool.

Reinstall system software.

Trouble

Unable to see any network devices.

Probable cause

Software settings not correct.

Extension conflicts.

Possible fix

Select Ethernet in the Network Control Panel and verify there are devices on the network.

Zap RAM. Hold down **Command-Option-P-R** during startup or use TechTool.

Turn off all unnecessary extensions and test.

Connect to a different Ethernet port.

If other users on the network are not experiencing trouble, you may need to replace the logic board.

Peripheral problems

Cursor or mouse problems

Trouble

Cursor does not move with the USB mouse.

Probable cause

USB connection faulty.

Dirty mouse.

Possible fix

Reconnect the mouse firmly into the USB keyboard.

Clean inside of mouse.

Attach mouse to other end of keyboard (replace keyboard if this works).

Replace mouse.

If nothing works, Apple recommends replacing the logic board.

Trouble

Cursor moves, but clicking USB mouse button has no effect.

Probable cause

Bad USB connection.

Possible fix

Disconnect mouse and place it on the other side of keyboard (if it works then replace the keyboard).

Replace USB mouse.

If nothing works, Apple recommends replacing the logic board.

Trouble

Double-click doesn't open application, disk, or server.

Probable cause

Extension conflict.

Possible duplicate system folders on hard drive.

Possible fix

Reboot with Extensions off or use Conflict Catcher.

Remove duplicate system folders if present.

Zap PRAM. Hold down **Command-Option-P-R** keys during startup or use TechTool.

Keyboard problems

Trouble

No response to any key on keyboard.

Probable cause

Bad USB connection.

Bad keyboard.

Possible fix

Reboot with extensions off.

Reseat USB connection to USB port on computer.

Attach another keyboard to the USB port to see if original is bad.

If nothing works, Apple recommends replacing the keyboard or logic board.

Printer problems

Trouble

USB printer does not work.

Probable cause

Drivers for printer corrupted or not present.

Printer not selected in Chooser.

USB connection not working.

Bad printer cable.

Possible fix

Reinstall printer drivers.

Select printer in Chooser if not already selected.

If printer is attached to a USB hub, disconnect and reconnect to the computer. If it works, hub is bad and should be replaced.

Turn off all unnecessary extensions and reboot.

Perform a clean install of the system software and print driver.

Replace printer interface cable.

Replace the printer if bad.

Trouble
>Network printer does not print.

Probable cause
>Printer drivers corrupted or not installed.

>Printer not selected in Chooser.

>Network connections down.

Possible fix
>Inspect network connections and reseat.

>Reinstall printer drivers.

>Select printer in Chooser if it is not already selected.

Trouble
>Cursor does not move with the ADB mouse.

Probable cause
>Mouse not firmly connected to keyboard, monitor or I/O ADB port.

>Dirty mouse.

Possible fix
>Take mouse out of keyboard and insert it into other side of keyboard. If it works then replace keyboard.

>If mouse still doesn't work, replace the mouse.

>If mouse and/or keyboard does not work when connected, Apple recommends replacing the logic board.

CD-ROM problems

Trouble
>CD-ROM tray won't open.

Probable cause
>CD-ROM drivers not present or corrupted.

CD-ROM data cable not attached to logic board.

Bad drive or disk.

Possible fix

Reinstall CD-ROM drivers.

Reseat cables on the back of drive.

Reseat CD-ROM data cable on the logic board.

Try another disk.

Replace the CD-ROM drive.

Trouble

CD-ROM icon does not appear on the desktop.

Probable cause

Software drivers bad or not present.

Cables not attached or faulty.

Possible fix

Reinstall CD-ROM drivers.

Reseat all cables from CD-ROM drive to computer.

Replace CD-ROM drive, or if nothing else works, replace the logic board.

Modem troubles

Trouble

The internal modem is not recognized.

Probable cause

Modem not seated properly.

Incorrect CCL and extension files or these are corrupted.

Modem cable not attached.

Possible fix

Reinstall all CCL and modem extension software.

Reinstall system software.

Reseat the modem cable on the logic board.

Zap PRAM. Hold down **Command-Option-P-R** or use TechTool.

Reseat the modem.

If nothing works, Apple recommends replacing the modem or the flexible modem cable.

Trouble
Modem reports an error when dialing out.

Probable cause
CCL or modem drivers not installed or corrupted.

Bad phone line.

Bad cable.

Possible fix
Reinstall all modem software.

Try another phone jack.

Try another phone cable.

Trouble
Computer freezes when modem dials.

Probable cause
Extensions conflict.

System software corrupted.

Possible fix
Use Conflict Catcher, or turn on only necessary extensions and modem drivers.

Reinstall system software.

Trouble
>
> Modem is having trouble connecting to online site.

Probable cause
> Bad phone lines.
>
> Bad TCP configuration.
>
> Host site is down.
>
> Wrong modem script.

Possible fix
> Use different phone jack.
>
> Use second line if you have one.
>
> Be sure configurations in the TCP/IP control panel are correct.
>
> Contact phone company if this happens with all calls.
>
> Contact Internet Provider if this happens just with Internet.

Trouble
> The system returns an error message when launching an internet browser.

Probable cause
> Software not installed correctly.

Possible fix
> With Internet Explorer 4 or later, use the Installer, not drag and drop.
>
> Reinstall Netscape Communicator software.

Trouble
> The dialup software will not initiate a connection.

Probable cause
> Software corrupted or not installed.
>
> Phone number not properly entered.

Possible fix

Reinstall software.

Ensure that a phone number is entered.

Trouble

Modem is dropping its connection.

Probable cause

Cracked phone wire or jack.

Bad external phone lines.

Host server having problems.

Modem not seated correctly or bad.

Possible fix

Try another phone cable or jack.

Connect at lower speed.

Contact phone company to test the line.

Turn off call waiting (enter *70 in modem script).

Contact host computer to see if they have problems.

Reseat the modem or replace.

Trouble

Modem disconnects after a period of time.

Probable cause

Online service or host computer has a time-out set for idle modems.

Possible fix

Check your Net software to see if a time-out period is set. Reset it or turn it off.

Contact the Net provider or host computer you are calling to see if they have a time-out set that is too short.

Trouble

Modem is slow responding.

Probable cause

High Net traffic.

Bad phone line (noise).

Modem is set for lower speeds.

Possible fix

Ensure that modem is set for highest possible speed.

Wait until a later time when your Net provider is not as busy.

Replace phone cable or have line tested.

Video/Monitor problems

Trouble

Screen is black.

Boot tone is heard.

Drive is spinning.

Fan is running.

LED is lit.

Probable cause

Bad video connection.

Bad monitor.

DIMMs not seated properly.

Jumpers wrong.

Possible fix

If using a VGA to MAC adapter, do not use one on each end of the supplied video cable to a monitor with a captive VGA connector, according to Apple.

Reseat video card and cables.

Reseat or replace DIMMs.

Check to see that jumper block configuration at J25 is correct. 300 MHz is black, 350 MHz is blue, and 400 MHz is white. If it is not correct, do not change it yourself this it will void Apple's warranty. Bring it to an Apple Certified Technician.

Zap PRAM. Hold down **Command-Option-P-R** during startup or use TechTool.

Replace the monitor cable.

Replace monitor (test by using another one on the computer).

If nothing works, Apple recommends resetting the Cuda chip or logic board, or replacing the logic board or processor module.

Trouble

Screen is black.

No boot sounds.

Drive not operating.

Fan is running.

LED is lit.

Probable cause

Bad video connection.

Jumpers not correct.

Video card not seated properly.

DIMMs not seated properly.

Possible fix

If using a VGA to MAC adapter do not use one on each end of the supplied video cable to a monitor with a captive VGA connector, according to Apple.

Check to see that jumper block configuration at J25 is correct. 300 MHz is black, 350 MHz is blue, and 400 MHz is white. If it is not correct, do not change it yourself since this will void Apple's warranty. Bring it to an Apple Certified Technician.

Make sure the metal jumper pins are in the correct position in the block and the block is installed in the correct direction.

Reseat the video card.

Reseat the DIMMs.

Reseat the processor module.

Reseat the DIMMs or replace defective ones.

Try another monitor cable.

If nothing works, Apple recommends resetting the Cuda chip or logic board, or replacing the video card, processor module, logic board, or power supply.

Trouble

Boot tone is heard.

Screen lights up.

Nothing is displayed on screen.

Probable cause

Bad video connection or cable.

PCI card not seated properly.

DIMMs not seated properly.

Possible fix

If using a VGA to MAC adapter do not use one on each end of the supplied video cable to a monitor with a captive VGA connector, according to Apple.

Reseat or replace PCI cards.

Reseat processor card.

Reseat DIMMs.

Try a different monitor cable.

If nothing works, Apple recommends resetting the Cuda chip or logic board, or replacing the processor module or logic board.

Trouble

Distorted video.

Probable cause

Bad video connection or cable.

Possible fix

Adjust the display's geometry if the monitor has adjustment settings you can access.

Replace the video cable or video adapter if you are using one.

Trouble

Erroneous text or characters appear on the screen.

Probable cause

Corrupted system software.

Keyboard connection defective.

Possible fix

Remove then reinsert keyboard connections.

Reinstall system software from the CD that came with your computer.

Replace keyboard.

Trouble

Flashing question mark on monitor.

Probable cause

Bad hard drive.

Bad external device on SCSI chain.

Bad or no system software on drive.

SCSI ID conflict.

Possible fix

Reinstall system software with CD that came with your computer.

Run Disk Aid or Norton Utilities.

Ensure that all SCSI devices have unique numbers.

Disconnect all external devices.

If nothing works, Apple recommends replacing the hard drive/CD data cable or hard drive.

Trouble

Screen jitters.

Probable cause

Video card not seated properly or defective.

Possible fix

Reseat the video card.

Replace the video card.

Zip drive problems

Trouble

Zip drive does not operate.

Probable cause

Bad Zip disk or drive.

Drive not getting power.

Zip drivers corrupted or not present.

Bad cables.

Possible fix

Try another Zip disk.

Reseat cables on the back of Zip drive.

Reinstall drivers.

Check device settings: device 0 (master), device 1 (slave).

Replace IDE/ATA drive cable.

Replace Zip drive.

If nothing works, Apple recommends replacing the logic board.

Trouble

During system startup, Zip disk ejects.

Probable cause/possible fix

Basically the same as previous.

Trouble

Zip disk does not eject.

Probable cause

Bad disk.

Bad drive or drivers corrupted.

Possible fix

Try another disk.

Switch off computer. Hold down mouse button while you switch computer on.

Reinstall Zip software.

If nothing works, Apple recommends replacing the Zip drive, IDE/ATA drive cable, or logic board.

Trouble

Zip drive attempts to eject disk, but doesn't succeed.

Probable cause

Zip drive bezel not aligned properly with drive.

Possible fix

Reseat the bezel so the slot aligns correctly.

Replace the drive.

Trouble

Zip drive runs continuously.

Probable cause

Bad disk or drive.

Software corrupted.

Possible fix

Try another disk.

Reinstall Zip drivers.

If nothing works, Apple recommends replacing the drive, IDE/ATA drive cable, or logic board.

G3 Server Model

Apple Systems startup problems

Trouble

Fan on power supply is running.

No startup chime.

Screen is black.

Drive not operational at startup.

No LED on front of system.

Probable cause

Bad voltage regulator.

Voltage set for wrong geographic area.

Jumper block not set correctly for the power supply installed or for processor module.

Possible fix

Inspect jumper block configuration at J28. Setting should be: 300 MHz is black, 350 MHz is blue, and 400 MHz is white. If it is not correct, do not change it yourself since this will void Apple's warranty. Bring it to an Apple Certified Technician.

Check jumper block configuration at J16. Correct color for processor type installed is: red jumper (233 MHz), white jumper (266 MHz), or black jumper (300 MHz), and be sure block is facing the right direction.

Reseat or replace voltage regulator.

Reseat processor module (locking arm in down position).

Reseat ROM DIMM.

If nothing works, Apple recommends replacing the logic board or processor module.

Trouble

Fan is running.

LED is on.

Drive is operational at startup.

No startup chime.

Screen is black.

Probable cause

ROM DIMM not seated properly.

Possible fix

Reseat ROM DIMM.

Trouble

No power.

Fan isn't running.

No LED on.

Probable cause

Power cord not secure.

Power outlet bad.

ADB cable is not seated properly or is bad.

Internal power cables not securely seated.

Possible fix

Reseat power cord; replace if bad.

Try another outlet.

Reseat ADB cable; replace if bad.

Reseat internal power cables.

Reseat voltage regulator.

Ensure power supply is set correctly for region.

Inspect jumper block configuration at J28. Setting should be: 300 MHz is black, 350 MHz is blue, and 400 MHz is white. If it is not correct, do not change it yourself since this will void Apple's warranty. Bring it to an Apple Certified Technician.

If nothing works, Apple recommends resetting the Cuda chip or logic board, or replacing the logic board.

Trouble

Computer begins to power up.

Fan is on.

Hard drive is operational.

Power LED is lit.

No video.

Boot chime sounds like breaking glass.

Probable cause

ROM DIMM not seated properly.

DRAM DIMMs not seated properly or defective.

External SCSI devices or cables not functioning.

Possible fix

Reseat ROM DIMM.

Reseat DRAM DIMMs. Replace if defective (test one at a time).

Inspect external SCSI cabling and reseat.

Ensure that all external SCSI devices are operational.

Trouble
Clicking, chirping, thumping, or rubbing sound.

Probable cause
PCI cards not seated properly.

Hard drive bad.

Floppy drive bad.

Possible fix
Reseat all PCI cards.

Remove hard drive and reboot. If problem stops, replace the hard drive.

Replace floppy drive cable.

Replace floppy drive.

If nothing works, Apple recommends replacing the power supply or processor module or replacing the I/O card.

Trouble
System shuts down intermittently.

Probable cause
Air flow restricted around computer.

Power cord not firmly connected.

Internal battery needs replacing.

Possible fix
Be sure ventilation around the computer is unrestricted. If the thermal protection circuit shut

down the computer, wait at least half an hour before restarting.

Reseat or replace power cord.

Replace battery.

If nothing works, Apple recommends resetting the Cuda chip or logic board, or replacing the power supply, logic board, or processor module.

Trouble

System intermittently crashes or hangs.

Probable cause

System software corrupt.

Extension conflict.

Application software being used is not compatible with computer or system version.

DIMMs not seated properly.

Possible fix

Ensure system software is version 8.0 or later with enabler 770 for G3 Minitower, or version 8.1 or later with appropriate software extensions for G3 Server.

Reinstall system software doing a clean install.

Be sure software used is Power Mac compatible.

Zap PRAM. Hold down **Command-Option-P-R** keys during startup or use TechTool.

Reseat all DIMMs. Replace defective ones (test one at a time).

If nothing happens, Apple recommends replacing the logic board or processor module.

Trouble

During startup, the following message is displayed on your monitor: "This startup disk will not work on this Macintosh model."

Probable cause

Corrupted system software on hard drive.

Startup disk is bad.

Possible fix

Try another startup disk.

Perform a clean install of system software.

Be sure you are using the correct version of system software and enabler 770 is present.

Ensure that you have appropriate software extensions for G3 server.

Trouble

Error chords.

One-part error chord (sound of breaking glass) sounds during startup sequence.

Probable cause

Bad hard drive.

Bad floppy drive.

Possible fix

Reseat IDE data cable from hard drive.

Reseat floppy drive cable.

Replace hard or floppy drive (test with a different one first).

Reseat the processor module.

If nothing works, Apple recommends replacing the logic board or processor module.

Audio (speaker) problems

Trouble

No sound from speaker.

Probable cause

Volume setting not correct (or mute is selected).

Microphone or external speakers connected.

Sound cable is not seated properly in logic board.

Bad speaker.

Possible fix

Adjust volume settings in control panel.

Disconnect microphone or external speakers and test.

Zap PRAM. Hold down **Command-Option-P-R** keys during startup or use TechTool.

Reseat cable from speaker into logic board.

Insert headphones or external speakers into the external jack.

If sound comes from the external jack, replace the internal speaker or logic board.

If the external jack does not emit sound, Apple recommends replacing the I/O audio card or logic board.

Floppy drive problems

Trouble

Internal floppy drive does not operate.

Probable cause

Bad disk in drive.

Floppy drive cable not seated or bad.

Bad floppy drive.

Possible fix

Try another floppy disk.

Reseat or replace floppy drive cable.

Replace floppy drive.

If nothing works, Apple recommends replacing the logic board or processor module.

Trouble

During system startup a floppy disk ejects from floppy drive and the monitor displays an icon with blinking "X".

Probable cause

Bad startup disk.

Bad floppy drive or cable.

Possible fix

Try another system disk.

Reseat or replace floppy drive cable.

Replace floppy drive.

If nothing works, Apple recommends replacing the logic board or processor module.

Trouble

Disk does not eject from floppy drive.

Probable cause

Bad disk, shutter stuck.

Floppy drive cable not seated or bad.

Bad floppy drive.

Possible fix

Eject disk manually by carefully inserting opened paper clip into hole near floppy drive slot.

Use keyboard shortcut **Cloverleaf-E**.

Use keyboard shortcut **Cloverleaf-Shift-1**.

Switch off computer. Hold down mouse button while you switch computer on.

Replace floppy drive cable or drive.

If nothing works, Apple recommends replacing the logic board or processor module.

Trouble

Floppy drive tries to eject disk, but disk does not come out.

Probable cause

Floppy drive bezel slots not aligned correctly.

Stuck floppy disk.

Bad floppy drive.

Possible fix

Reseat floppy drive bezel and drive to realign slots.

Manually remove disk.

Replace floppy drive.

Trouble

MS-DOS drive does not recognize a disk formatted on a 1.4 MB drive.

Probable cause

Floppy disks not formatted on MS-DOS drive.

Possible fix

Format all disks on the MS-DOS drive first.

Hard drive problems

Trouble

Single internal hard drive does not operate (drive isn't spinning).

Probable cause

Bad hard drive power cable.

Bad hard drive.

Possible fix

Reseat or replace hard drive power cable.

Replace hard drive.

If nothing works, Apple recommends replacing the power supply.

Trouble

No internal SCSI drives are operating.

Probable cause

SCSI ID conflict.

Termination is wrong on the SCSI chain.

Bad drives.

Possible fix

Inspect and ensure that all devices have unique SCSI ID number.

Disconnect any external SCSI devices and see if they are terminated properly (only last device in SCSI chain should be terminated).

Reseat or replace internal SCSI data cable that is connected to the device not working.

If nothing works, Apple recommends replacing the power supply, logic board, or processor module.

Trouble

Computer works with internal or external SCSI devices but not with both.

Probable cause

SCSI ID conflict.

Termination of SCSI chain not correct.

Possible fix

Ensure that all SCSI devices have a unique SCSI ID number.

Check terminator on external device and replace if necessary

Ensure that only the last SCSI device on the chain is terminated.

Network (Ethernet) problems

Trouble

Ethernet connection drops off line by itself.

Probable cause

Incorrect Ethernet driver.

Possible fix

Install Ethernet driver 2.0.4 or later.

Peripheral problems

Cursor or mouse problems

Trouble

Cursor on screen does not move.

Probable cause

Dirty mouse.

ADB connection is loose or cable is bad on computer ADB port or keyboard.

Possible fix

Clean mouse.

Reseat ADB connection.

Connect mouse to different ADB port instead. If mouse works, replace keyboard.

Reseat or replace ADB cable.

Replace mouse if it does not work on any ADB port.

If nothing works, Apple recommends replacing the logic board or processor module.

Trouble

Cursor moves on screen, but clicking mouse button has no effect.

Probable cause

Bad mouse.

Software conflict.

Possible fix

Restart computer from floppy or bootable CD.

Reinstall system software.

Replace mouse.

Trouble

Double-clicking the mouse doesn't open application, disk, or server.

Probable cause

There is more than one system folder on the hard drive.

Software conflict.

ADB connection is faulty.

Possible fix

Remove duplicate system folders if they exist.

Zap PRAM. Hold down **Command-Option-P-R** keys during startup or use TechTool.

Connect mouse to different ADB port if on keyboard. If it works, then replace the keyboard.

Replace ADB cable.

Clean mouse.

If mouse fails on all ADB port connections, replace the mouse.

If nothing works, Apple recommends replacing the logic board.

Keyboard problems

Trouble

No response at all to any key on keyboard.

Probable cause

ADB connection is loose or faulty.

Bad keyboard or cable.

Possible fix

Reseat ADB connection.

Replace ADB keyboard cable.

Replace keyboard.

If nothing works, Apple recommends replacing the logic board.

Printer problems

Trouble

The serial printer does not work.

Probable cause

Printer drivers corrupted or not installed.

Printer not selected in Chooser.

System software corrupted.

Printer cable bad or not seated properly.

Possible fix

Reinstall printer drivers.

Perform clean install of system software.

Be sure that system software and printer driver versions are compatible (check with printer vendor).

Reseat or replace printer interface cable.

If nothing works, Apple recommends replacing the logic board.

Trouble

The network printer does not print.

Probable cause

Network connection is broken.

Printer drivers corrupted or not installed.

Printer not selected in Chooser.

System software corrupted.

Possible fix

Inspect network connections and correct if broken.

Select printer in Chooser.

Reinstall printer drivers or clean install system software.

Ensure printer driver and system software are compatible (check printer vendor).

If nothing works, Apple recommends replacing the logic board.

Trouble

Color StyleWriter 4500 printer does not work.

Probable cause

Corrupted or outdated printer driver.

Possible fix

Install Color StyleWriter 4500 driver, version 1.1 or later, which you can obtain from Apple's Web site at **http://www.apple.com/support/**.

CD-ROM problems

Trouble

CD-ROM drive does not work.

Probable cause

Bad disk.

CD-ROM drivers corrupted or not installed.

CD-ROM data cable not seated properly or bad.

Bad CD-ROM drive.

Possible fix

Try another disk.

Reinstall CD-ROM drivers.

Reseat CD-ROM data cable at logic board connector as well as at CD-ROM connector.

Replace CD-ROM data cable.

Replace the CD-ROM drive.

Trouble

Macintosh does not display CD-ROM icon once CD is inserted in drive.

Probable cause

Bad disk.

CD-ROM drivers corrupted or not installed.

CD-ROM data cable not seated properly or bad.

Possible fix

Try another disk.

Reinstall CD-ROM drivers.

Reseat CD-ROM data cable at logic board connector as well as at CD-ROM connector.

Replace CD-ROM data cable.

Replace CD-ROM drive.

Video/monitor problems

Trouble

Screen is black.

Boot tone heard.

Drive operates.

Fan is running.

LED is on.

Probable cause

Monitor's brightness control not correct.

Monitor cable not seated properly or defective.

DIMMs bad or not seated correctly.

Bad monitor.

Possible fix

Use brightness control and adjust.

Zap PRAM. Hold down **Command-Option-P-R** keys or use TechTool.

Replace monitor cable.

Reseat or replace DIMMs.

Replace bad monitor (try another one first).

If nothing works, Apple recommends resetting the Cuda chip or logic board or replacing the logic board, or processor module.

Trouble

Screen is black.

No boot tone.

Drive not working.

Fan is running.

LED is lit.

Probable cause

DIMMs bad or not seated properly.

Possible fix

Reseat or replace DIMMs (test one at time).

If this does not work, Apple recommends resetting the Cuda chip or logic board, or replacing the logic board, power supply, or processor module.

Trouble

Boot tone is heard.

Screen lights up.

Nothing shows up on screen.

Probable cause

Bad monitor cable or monitor.

Possible fix

Reseat or replace monitor cable.

Try another monitor.

Replace defective monitor.

If nothing works, Apple recommends resetting the Cuda chip or logic board.

Trouble

Horizontal flickering lines visible on monitor.

Probable cause

Apple Video Play application with video mirroring on.

Possible fix

Apple recommends replacing the Audio/Video card with a Version II Audio/Video card (p/n 661-2044).

G3 Powerbook Series

Apple Systems startup problems

Trouble

On startup RAM failure occurs.

The sound of breaking glass is heard after the startup chord.

Probable cause

Bad DIMMs, microprocessor board, or I/O board.

Possible fix

Reseat DIMMs.

If top RAM SODIMM exists, remove and restart computer.

If startup sequence is normal, replace RAM SODIMM.

Remove bottom SODIMM and restart. If the computer starts up fine this time, RAM DIMMs were not seated properly.

If RAM SODIMMs are fine and machine continues to fail, Apple recommends replacing the microprocessor or I/O logic board.

Trouble

Hardware failure occurs.

A four-tone error chord sequence is audible after the startup chord.

Probable cause

Bad hard drive, hard drive connector board, I/O, or microprocessor board.

Possible fix

Power down the computer and disconnect any external devices.

Reboot and Zap PRAM. Hold down **Command-Option-P-R** keys until the second startup tone is heard).

Remove any expansion modules in the left or right expansion bay, and restart computer. If startup sequence is normal, reinsert expansion modules one at a time and retest.

Replace defective module.

Disconnect hard drive connector and restart computer. If startup sequence is normal, reconnect cable and retest. If not, replace cable or hard drive.

If none of these works, Apple recommends replacing the I/O logic or microprocessor board.

Trouble

Computer won't power up.

Probable cause

Bad sound card.

Bad power supply.

Bad PMU card.

Cables not seated properly.

I/O logic or microprocessor board not seated or bad.

Microprocessor card not seated or bad.

Bad keyboard.

Possible fix

Reseat both ends of power adapter.

Try a different power adapter.

If the sleep LED is continually on, restart computer by holding down **Shift-FN-Control** and **Power On** key. Wait a few seconds and restart. Try this several times.

Try new battery.

Disconnect keyboard and power up. Replace keyboard if machine powers up.

If nothing works, Apple recommends replacing the sound card, power supply card, PMU card, I/O logic board, or microprocessor board.

Trouble

Screen is blank.

Backlight is off.

No response from computer.

Probable cause

Backup battery power interrupted.

Bad power adapter.

Dead battery.

Loose cable.

Possible fix

Restart computer by holding down **Shift-FN-Control** and **Power On** key if sleep LED is continually on. Try several times.

Disconnect power adapter, remove battery, and restart computer in 3–4 minutes.

Reseat the power adapter cable.

Try a new or other charged battery.

Disconnect backup battery for 2 minutes. Reconnect and reboot.

Make sure all I/O logic board cables and connections are firm inside.

If nothing works, you may have to replace the sound card, microprocessor board, power supply card, PMU card, or I/O logic board.

Trouble

Some Control Panel settings changed after the battery was removed.

Probable cause

Backup battery needs to be recharged or cable is not firmly seated.

Possible fix

Charge the backup battery for a full 48 hours.

Connect power adapter for 24 hours.

Inspect and reseat the backup battery cable and connections.

If nothing works, Apple recommends replacing the backup battery, PMU card, cable from PMU to I/O logic board, or the I/O logic board.

Trouble

Power adapter is plugged in but Control Strip doesn't indicate adapter is connected.

Probable cause

Power adapter bad or no power at the outlet.

Possible fix

Make sure the power adapter is firmly seated.

Try a new power adapter.

Make sure there is power coming from the outlet.

If nothing works, you may need to replace the sound card PMU card or cable, or I/O logic board.

Trouble

Computer runs when plugged into wall outlet but not on battery power.

Probable cause

Battery not seated properly.

Battery dead.

Bad I/O logic board or power supply.

Possible fix

Reset power manager (**shift-Fn-Ctrl-Pwr** button).

Check battery shims. According to Apple, battery shims are adhesive strips mounted on the battery to make sure it fits properly.

Apple says the number of battery shims needed depends on the battery serial number. Serial numbers ending with either AXW or E7L require three shims (on each side and the bottom). Serial numbers ending with E3W or E7M require one shim (bottom only). Do not remove them unless you are replacing them.

Take out the battery and put it back in to make sure it's connecting with contacts on I/O logic board.

Insert the battery in opposite expansion bay.

Try a new or other fully charged battery.

Try another power adapter.

If nothing works, Apple recommends replacing the charge card, PMU board, power supply card, or I/O logic board.

Trouble

Premature low-power warning appears.

Probable cause

Battery not fully charged.

Possible fix

Try using a different power adapter or fully charged battery.

If problem persists, Apple recommends replacing the sound card, PMU board or cable or both, power supply card, or I/O logic board.

Trouble

Battery won't charge.

Probable cause

Bad battery.

EMI shield touching power adapter shield preventing charging.

Possible fix

Reset power manager (**shift-Fn-Ctrl-Pwr** button).

Try battery in opposite expansion bay.

Make sure EMI shield isn't in contact with outer shield of the power adapter.

Replace battery.

If nothing works, Apple recommends replacing the charge card, PMU board, power supply card, or I/O logic board.

Trouble

Battery will not charge unless unit is in sleep mode or shut down.

Probable cause

Power adapter not firmly seated.

EMI shield in contact with power adapter's outer shield.

Possible fix

Make sure power adapter is firmly connected.

Inspect the EMI shield for contact with outer shield of the power adapter.

Try a new or other good battery.

If nothing works, Apple recommends replacing the charge card, PMU board, power supply card, or I/O logic board.

Video

Trouble

Partial or full row of pixels is always on or never comes on in an active matrix display.

Probable cause

Display cables or connections broken.

Possible fix

Reseat or replace display cables and connections.

If that does not work, Apple recommends replacing the I/O logic board.

Trouble

Display is very light or totally white.

Probable cause

Adjustments off.

Connections or cable broken.

Possible fix

Adjust screen contrast (FSTN units only) and brightness settings.

Reseat data cable to I/O logic board connection, inverter board connection, and I/O logic board connections.

If nothing works, Apple recommends replacing the I/O logic board.

Trouble

An external monitor connected to the PowerBook shows no video.

Probable cause

External monitor bad or doesn't have power.

Video adapter not working.

Possible fix

Try another video adapter or monitor.

Make sure monitor is getting power.

Restart unit and reset PRAM.

If nothing works, Apple recommends replacing the I/O logic board.

Trouble

No display.

Computer appears to operate correctly.

Probable cause

Screen adjustment may be off.

Cables and connections unseated.

Possible fix

Reset power manager if sleep light is blinking but computer is not in sleep mode.

Insert disk into floppy drive and eject it with the **Command-E** keys to verify that computer is working.

Adjust the screen brightness setting.

Reseat display cable, inverter board, PMU connections, and I/O logic board connections.

If nothing works, Apple recommends replacing the inverter board, display, or I/O logic board.

Trouble

Backlight doesn't operate.

Probable cause

Adjustments off.

Cable and connections unseated.

Possible fix

Readjust screen brightness setting.

Reseat the backlight cable connection, display cable, inverter board and cable, and I/O logic board connections. Make sure all cables are good and not pinched or broken.

If nothing works, Apple recommends replacing the I/O logic board or display.

Trouble

Screen flickers or shows intermittent vertical lines.

Probable cause

Display cable loose.

Possible fix

Apple says to squeeze the upper left side of the display bezel. If the problem disappears, a display cable replacement is needed.

Audio problems

Trouble

No sound from speaker(s).

Settings not correct.

Bad sound card or cable.

Possible fix

Be sure the mute mode is not enabled and the volume setting is above 0.

Check to see that there are no external speakers or headphones plugged in.

Make sure speaker cable is plugged into sound card.

If nothing works, Apple recommends replacing the sound card, speaker(s), or I/O logic board.

Floppy drive problems

Trouble

Audio and video are present.

Floppy drive in expansion bay does not operate.

Probable cause

Disk not inserted correctly.

Floppy drive not seated.

Expansion bay not working.

Possible fix

Make sure the floppy disk is inserted correctly in the drive.

Put the floppy drive in opposite expansion bay.

Start the system with extensions off.

Insert one or more other floppy disks to see if it is the drive and not the disk.

Reseat floppy drive.

Put the floppy drive in the opposite expansion bay.

If nothing works, Apple recommends replacing the floppy drive or I/O logic board.

Trouble

Read/write/copy error.

Probable cause

Bad floppy drive.

Bad disks.

Possible fix

Try several other good floppy disks.

Restart with extensions off.

Attempt to format a floppy disk.

If nothing works, Apple recommends replacing the floppy drive or the I/O logic board.

Trouble
    Disk does not eject.

Probable cause
    Bad floppy drive.

    Bad disk.

Possible fix
    Be sure the floppy disk is inserted squarely in the drive.

    Put the floppy drive in the opposite expansion bay.

    If floppy drive is in the right expansion bay, switch off system and hold down **Command-Shift-1** while you restart.

    If floppy drive is in the left expansion bay, switch off system and hold down **Command-Shift-2** while you restart.

    Eject disk manually by carefully inserting opened paper clip into hole near floppy drive slot.

    If nothing works, Apple recommends replacing the floppy drive or I/O logic board.

Trouble
    Disk initialization fails.

Probable cause
    Bad floppy drive or disk.

    Bad expansion bay.

    Extensions conflict.

Possible fix
    Try another floppy.

    Be sure floppy is inserted squarely and correctly in the drive.

    Insert the floppy drive in opposite expansion bay and retest.

Boot up with extensions off.

If nothing happens, Apple recommends replacing the floppy drive or I/O logic board.

Hard drive problems

Trouble

Internal hard drive does not spin.

Probable cause

No power to drive.

SCSI ID conflict.

Connections and cables not seated properly.

Possible fix

Disconnect all SCSI devices and reboot.

Ensure all SCSI devices have unique SCSI ID number.

Reseat all cables and connections to the hard drive.

Be sure there is power going to the computer.

If nothing works, Apple recommends replacing the hard drive or I/O logic board.

CD-ROM drive/DVD-ROM drive

Trouble

CD-ROM or DVD-ROM drive does not accept disk.

Probable cause

Dirty or defective disk.

Bad drive.

Bad I/O logic board.

Apple CD extensions not present.

Possible fix

Check to see if Apple CD extensions are on. If not,

turn on or reinstall.

Be sure CD drive is seated correctly and connections are tight.

Check another disk to see if first one is damaged.

If nothing works, Apple recommends replacing the drive or I/O logic board.

Trouble
Volume control does not operate correctly.

Probable cause
Settings not correct.

Possible fix
Verify that the Control Panel Sound settings are correct and that the mute mode is not selected.

Turn volume control button up.

Reinsert drive and check connections.

Trouble
Macintosh cannot mount drive.

Probable cause
Bad drive or I/O logic board.

Drivers not correct or corrupted.

Possible fix
Reinstall drivers.

Reseat drive and check all connections.

If nothing works, Apple recommends replacing the drive or I/O logic board.

Trouble
Audio and video are present.

Drive in expansion bay does not operate.

Probable cause

Defective drive.

Bad expansion bay.

Apple CD extensions not installed or corrupted.

Possible fix

Reinstall Apple CD extensions.

Try another CD to make sure it is not a defective disk.

If nothing works, Apple recommends replacing the drive.

PC card module (PCMCIA) problems

Trouble

PC card won't eject.

Probable cause

Computer is in sleep mode.

PC card is not inserted correctly.

Possible fix

Awake computer if in sleep.

Drag PC card to trash can and reinsert.

Power down the computer and try the PC card eject buttons.

Eject disk manually by carefully inserting opened paper clip into hole near floppy drive slot.

Remove the top of the case and gently push on the PC card while ejecting it.

Replace the card with a new one if it is damaged.

Trouble

PC card is inserted but doesn't appear on desktop.

Probable cause

Damaged card or slot.

Software drivers not installed or damaged.

Possible fix

Insert the PC card in the other slot.

Reinstall the software drivers for the card.

If nothing works, Apple recommends replacing the PC card, PC card cardcage, or I/O logic board.

Apple says that if "defective card" or "unrecognizable card" appears in place of card name in PCMCIA Eject control panel, card is damaged or computer does not have software required to support it. Eject card. Modem and communication cards may not appear on desktop.

Trouble

PC card can't be inserted.

Probable cause

PC card cardcage is damaged.

Bad card.

PC card is not being inserted properly.

Bad slot.

Possible fix

Perform a soft eject and wait 8 seconds for the cardcage to reset.

Be sure to insert PC card from center, not off center.

Check a different PC card to make sure the problem is the card.

Insert card into the other slot to see if it is a bad slot.

If nothing works, Apple recommends replacing the PC card cardcage.

Trouble

PC card flies out of cardcage when ejected.

Probable cause

Cardcage is out of alignment

Possible fix

Install another PC card to see if the card is defective.

If nothing works, Apple recommends a realignment of the PC card cardcage so that PC card tracks are parallel.

DVD-Video PC card problems

Trouble

DVD-Video PC card icon does not appear on desktop, or generic PC card icon (without the word "DVD") appears on desktop.

Probable cause

Bad card.

DVD software is missing or corrupted or not enabled (use Extensions Manager to turn on).

Possible fix

Reinstall software from Apple DVD software CD.

Check the DVD-Video PC card to make sure it is firmly inserted in lower PC card slot.

Power down the computer and manually eject DVD-Video PC card. Wait 15 seconds and insert card again.

Try another PC card in lower slot to see if upper slot is bad.

If nothing works, Apple recommends replacing the DVD-Video PC card or the PC card cardcage.

Trouble

DVD-Video disk will not play.

Probable cause

Bad disk.

DVD-Video PC card is not seated properly.

Parental Controls Settings not correct.

Possible fix

Check that the DVD-Video PC card is inserted in lower PC card slot, eject and reinsert.

Try another DVD disk to make sure it is not a bad disk.

Check to see if Parental Controls setting is set to "on." Select an MPAA rating at the same level or higher than the title being viewed.

Check region code for DVD-Video title. (Warning message appears.) According to Apple, some DVD video disks can only play in a specific geographical region. For example, disks from Region 1 (US and Canada) cannot be played by a card purchased in Region 4 (Mexico and South America), and vice versa.

Trouble

Movie plays, but special features (such as director's notes, other languages, etc.) are unavailable.

Probable cause

Those features not available on the disk.

Apple DVD software may be corrupted.

Bad card (if the picture and sound are okay, the DVD-video PC card is fine).

Possible fix

Try another title to see if the disk is defective.

Reinstall the Apple DVD software CD.

Trouble

Poor performance of DVD video disk (poor sound or picture).

Probable cause

DVD disk is damaged or scratched.

Virtual memory is on.

"Power Cycling" and "Reduced Processor Speed" are set in the advanced settings of the Energy Saver Control Panel.

Extension conflict.

Possible fix

Inspect disk for scratches or damage.

Try another disk.

Turn Virtual Memory off.

Turn "Power Cycling" and "Reduced Processor Speed" in the Energy Saver control panel advanced settings off.

Turn off all extensions other than the standard Apple extensions and DVD extensions and restart.

Infrared communication problems

Trouble

Infrared communication is not working.

Probable cause

Infrared window dirty or blocked.

Other infrared devices are out of range or at wrong angle.

Host computer may not be receiving the infrared signal.

Possible fix

Clean the infrared window with soft lint-free cloth.

Be sure that devices are located at a distance greater than three but less than six feet. Angles must be less than 20 degrees.

If nothing works, Apple recommends replacing the I/O logic board.

Modem problems

Trouble

No dial tone.

Probable cause

Telephone line not working.

Modem cable is inserted in wrong port on the computer.

Bad modem.

Possible fix

Try another phone jack.

Reinsert cable into modem port located on the left in front of the PC card doors.

Using Apple Remote Access 3.0, select Ignore Dial Tone in the modem control panel.

Reset modem to default settings by entering OK in a terminal session.

Replace modem.

Trouble

No internal modem selection available.

Probable cause

No internal modem in computer.

Modem connections faulty.

Modem software installed or selected.

Possible fix

Be sure there is a modem in the computer and it is properly connected.

Reinstall and select modem software.

If nothing works, Apple recommends replacing the modem.

Peripheral problems

Trouble

After external SCSI device is connected, computer does not boot.

Probable cause

Bad SCSI cable or connections.

SCSI ID settings are set to the same number as another device.

SCSI chain is not terminated correctly.

Possible fix

Check the SCSI ID of all devices connected and be sure each has a different number.

Terminate the daisy chain correctly.

Try a different cable and check connections and cable.

If nothing works, Apple recommends replacing the I/O logic board.

Trouble

Serial device such as digital camera not recognized by computer

Probable cause

Wrong version of the DMA extension.

Bad serial port.

Bad camera.

Possible fix

Install Serial DMA extension version 2.1 or higher.

Turn off AppleTalk.

Begin download command on camera software then turn on camera.

Turn on camera after initiating download with camera application.

Try a different serial device on same port to see if defect is in camera or port.

If nothing works, Apple recommends replacing the I/O logic board.

Trouble

Cursor does not move when you are using track-pad.

Probable cause

Bad trackpad or connections.

Keyboard connections faulty.

Possible fix

Reseat trackpad and keyboard connections.

Power down computer and remove both adapter and battery. Restart after a minute or two.

Reset power manager.

Connect a mouse and see if the cursor moves. If it does, you need to replace the trackpad. If mouse does not work, you need to replace the PMU board.

Connect low-power mouse and try to move cursor. If trackpad does not move cursor but external ADB mouse does, replace trackpad. If external ADB mouse also doesn't move, replace PMU board.

If nothing works, Apple recommends replacing the I/O logic board.

Trouble

Cursor intermittently does not move or moves erratically.

Probable cause

Dirty trackpad.

Trackpad connections faulty.

Possible fix

Clean the trackpad using a non-static cloth.

Reset the power manager.

Reseat all connections to trackpad.

If nothing works, Apple recommends replacing the trackpad, trackpad cable, PMU card, or I/O logic board.

Trouble

Cursor moves, but clicking trackpad button has no effect.

Probable cause

Bad trackpad, cable or connections.

Possible fix

Reset Power Manager.

Reseat trackpad connections and cables.

If nothing works, Apple recommends replacing the trackpad, PMU card, or I/O logic board.

Trouble

Cursor does not move when mouse is in use.

Probable cause

Mouse is plugged into S-Video instead of ADB port.

Bad mouse.

Possible fix

Try another good mouse. If it works, you have a dead mouse; replace it.

Reseat the mouse connection to the ADB port. Make sure it is firm.

Clean mouse ball and inside of mouse.

If nothing works, Apple recommends replacing the I/O logic board.

Trouble

No response to any key on keyboard.

Probable cause

Keyboard connections and cable faulty.

Computer is not on.

Possible fix

Turn on the computer.

Reset the power manager by restarting the computer as you hold down **Shift-FN-Control-Power On** keys.

Reseat keyboard connections.

If nothing works Apple recommends replacing the keyboard, keyboard cable, PMU card, or I/O logic board.

Printing problems

Trouble

Direct-connect printer does not print.

Probable cause

Printer not selected in Chooser.

Parameter RAM scrambled.

Cables not connected or faulty.

Possible fix

Select the printer in the chooser.

Make AppleTalk inactive and select the modem port if printer and modem port appear separately.

Make AppleTalk inactive in the AppleTalk control panel under Options and restart unit.

Reset PRAM.

Reseat cables.

Replace printer cable.

If nothing works, Apple recommends replacing the I/O logic board.

Trouble

Network printer does not print.

Probable cause

Break in the network.

Chooser and Control Panel settings are not correct.

Cables are faulty or not seated properly.

Possible fix

Reset PRAM.

Go to Chooser and Control Panel and select the printer correctly.

Reinstall the printer drivers.

Replace cables.

Connect the printer directly to the computer.

If nothing works, Apple recommends replacing the I/O logic board.

Trouble

I/O devices are unrecognized, or garbage is transmitted or received.

Probable cause

Cables or connections faulty.

Bad SCSI termination.

Bad drivers.

Possible fix

Reset PRAM.

Reseat cables (use Apple cables).

Be sure the SCSI device is correctly terminated and there is a unique SCSI ID selected.

Reinstall drivers or download updated ones from vendor.

Test device with another computer to make sure it is the device that is faulty.

If nothing works, Apple recommends replacing the I/O logic board.

Trouble

In disk mode, computer does not display SCSI icon until host is booted, or computer crashes when host is shut down.

Probable cause

SCSI ID conflict.

Bad cable.

Possible fix

Ensure that all SCSI devices have unique numbers.

Reseat or replace SCSI disk mode cable.

Check security password is off.

If nothing works, Apple recommends replacing the I/O board.

Miscellaneous

Trouble

Sleep light won't come on.

Probable cause

Computer not in sleep mode.

Control buttons cable bad or not seated properly.

Possible fix

Reseat or replace control buttons cable.

Zap the PRAM.

If that doesn't work, Apple recommends resetting the Power Manager.

Trouble

Screen goes blank and computer shuts down every few minutes.

Probable cause

Computer is going into system sleep to conserve battery power.

Possible fix

Go into the Energy Saver Control Panel and adjust the sleep delays.

Plug in the power adapter.

Trouble

Application seems to run slower after a few seconds.

Probable cause

Computer is switching to system rest.

Possible fix

Connect power adapter.

Open the Energy Saver Control Panel under Advanced Settings and turn off processor cycling.

Trouble

Hard drive is slow to respond, or screen goes blank too often.

Probable cause

Energy Saver Control Panel not set correctly.

Possible fix

Connect the power adapter.

Go into the Energy Saver Control Panel and adjust the sleep delays.

Trouble

Intermittent operating problems such as no booting or initialization errors.

Probable cause

Microprocessor board not installed or seated properly.

Possible fix

Press all around on microprocessor board to make sure the board is fully seated.

iMac Troubleshooting

Important Note: On earlier iMac models (A, B, and C), memory modules (RAM) must be of the SDRAM SODIMM type whereas the DV models require the PC100 type. They don't mix!

Apple Mac System startup problems

Trouble

No power.

No LED.

No fan heard.

No hard drive power.

Screen is black.

Probable cause

Power cord is not seated correctly, bad, or outlet is dead.

Keyboard is dead.

Possible fix

Reseat Power cord, replace if defective.

Try another outlet.

Reseat the keyboard connection.

Power on computer from startup button on computer after disconnecting keyboard.

If power up occurs, replace the keyboard.

If nothing works, Apple recommends resetting the CUDA chip or logic board, or replacing the logic board, power/headphone board, power filter board, or power supply.

Error beep(s)

Trouble

One error beep at startup.

Probable cause

No DRAM is installed or detected, or DRAM is defective.

Possible fix

Reseat the SDRAM.

Replace defective SDRAM.

Trouble

Two beeps at startup.

Probable cause

Incompatible RAM is installed.

Possible fix

Be sure that SDRAM SODIMMs are installed on early iMacs, PC 100 on DV models, and not EDO modules.

Replace if wrong kind.

Trouble

Three beeps at startup.

Probable cause

Bad RAM.

Possible fix

Replace the existing SDRAM one DIMM at a time and replace the defective one.

Trouble

Four or five beeps at startup.

Probable cause

Bad ROM.

Defective processor module.

Possible fix

Reseat the processor module, or replace if bad.

If nothing works, Apple recommends replacing the logic board.

Flashing question mark

Trouble

You see nothing but a flashing question mark on the screen during start-up.

Probable cause

Corrupted system software or software drivers.

Hard drive cables not seated correctly.

Bad hard drive.

Possible fix

Reboot with the system CD that came with the iMac. If it boots up, reinstall the system software.

Reinstall the drivers.

Reinitialize the hard drive (all data will be lost).

Reseat the hard drive data or power cable or replace if defective.

If nothing works, Apple recommends replacing the hard drive.

System hangs (freezes) during startup

Trouble

System boots normally but iMac freezes before you get to the finder.

Probable cause

Extension conflict.

Corrupted system software.

Bad SDRAM.

Loose cables on the hard drive.

Bad hard drive.

External device bad (SCSI or USB).

Possible fix

Restart the computer with extensions off (hold down the **Shift** key during startup).

If it starts up, and you just installed new software, see if it placed an extension in the Extensions folder and remove it. Restart. If it starts fine, get a newer version of the extension from the software company.

Or disable all extensions then return one extension at a time to find the culprit.

Reboot from the system CD that came with your computer. It if boots up, replace the system software from the CD that came with your computer

Reseat or replace the SDRAM if defective.

Reinstall the drivers for the hard drive.

Reinitialize the hard drive (all data will be lost).

Reseat or replace hard drive cables.

Disconnect external devices and reattach one at a time. Replace the culprit.

If nothing works, Apple recommends replacing the hard drive.

Trouble

Periodically the iMac just freezes while you are working.

Probable cause

Extension conflict.

Corrupted system software.

Bad USB device or not seated properly.

Defective memory modules.

Possible fix

Restart the computer with extensions off (hold down the **Shift** key during startup).

If it starts up, and you just installed new software see if it placed an extension in the Extensions folder and remove it. Restart. If it starts fine, get a newer version of the extension from the software company.

Troubleshoot extensions.

Reinstall the system software from the CD that came with your computer.

Shut down and disconnect all USB peripherals. Restart using the startup button on the front of the iMac (won't work on iMac model A).

Reattach each peripheral until you find the culprit. Replace.

Reseat the memory module or replace if defective.

If nothing works, Apple recommends replacing the logic board or processor module.

Trouble

You see the following dialog box: "The built-in memory test has detected a problem. Please contact a service provider for assistance."

Probable cause
Bad SDRAM.

Possible fix
Reseat or replace defective SDRAM SODIMM.

Trouble
iMac cannot be awakened from sleep.

Green or amber LED on.

Probable cause
System software corrupted.

PRAM corrupted.

If LED is green, a bad analog/video board.

Possible fix
Zap PRAM. Hold down **Command-Option-P-R** keys when restarting or use TechTool.

Reinstall system software from the CD that came with the iMac.

If nothing works, replace the analog/video board.

Trouble
iMac (model A) does not force restart using key combinations or Power button on front panel when it freezes.

Probable cause
Bad design.

Possible fix
Unplug the power cord from behind and plug it back in. You lost whatever you were working on unless the software application made an automatic backup (Word and WordPerfect do this).

Use a straightened out paperclip and insert it in the reset hole on the side panel (this does not always work).

Purchase an ibutton from Joseph Lee and place it over the Reset button (**www.imacbutton.com**).

Audio problems

Sound out problems

Trouble

No sound emitted from internal or external speakers.

Probable cause

Volume settings on mute or off.

Bad internal or external speakers.

Speaker cables not seated properly or bad.

Possible fix

Check control panel settings and adjust.

Disconnect microphones, speakers, headphones and try each item for culprit.

Zap RAM. Hold down **Command-Option-P-R** keys during startup or use TechTool.

Reseat the audio cable at the A/V interconnect board and the power/headphone board.

Replace the audio cable that connects to location J14 on the logic board and at location J1 on the A/V interconnect board or the audio cable that connects the internal speakers to the A/V interconnect board and power/headphone board.

Check for sound coming out of the external jack.

If nothing works, Apple recommends replacing the logic board.

Sound in problems

Trouble

No sound recorded when using microphone.

The quality of the sound is bad.

You hear a high degrees of "noise."

Probable cause

Control settings incorrect.

Cables not seated properly.

Bad microphone.

Possible fix

Adjust the sound control panel by choosing CD quality under the Sound menu.

Reseat or replace the 5-connector audio cable on the outside of the A/V Interconnect board.

Install a new microphone gasket on the front bezel that surrounds the microphone input.

Trouble

No sound emitted from internal or external speakers.

Probable cause

Control settings incorrect.

Cables not seated properly.

Bad microphone.

Possible fix

Adjust the sound control panel by choosing CD quality under the Sound menu.

Reseat or replace the 5-connector audio cable on the outside of the A/V Interconnect board.

Install a new microphone gasket on the front bezel that surrounds the microphone input.

CD-ROM problems

Trouble

CD-ROM not showing on desktop.

Can't open CD.

CD-ROM vibrates.

Probable cause

Bad CD disc.

System software bad.

CD-ROM cable not seated properly.

Bad CD-ROM drive.

CD-ROM drive lens dirty.

Possible fix

Try another CD disc to verify that it is or is not disc.

Some vibration is noisy. If you have the original iMac Rev A or B, use the iMac CD Update v.10 to update the firmware on your CD-ROM drive (**www.apple.com**).

Reinstall system software from the CD that came with your computer.

Reseat CD-ROM drive cable at both ends or replace if defective.

Clean the CD-ROM drive lens.

If nothing works, Apple recommends replacing the CD-ROM drive or logic board.

Trouble

CD-ROM door not latching closed (both Rev A and B iMacs).

Probable cause

Bad CD-ROM disc.

CD-ROM tray eject device stuck.

Possible fix

Stick a straightened out paperclip into the eject mechanism to reset.

Replace the CD-ROM drive.

Hard drive problems

Trouble

Hard drive does not appear on the desktop. No evidence that it is spinning.

Probable cause

Corrupted System software.

Corrupted drivers.

Bad hard drive.

Bad hard drive cables or they are not seated properly.

Possible fix

Reinstall system software.

Reinstall drivers.

Reinitialize hard drive using drive setup that came with your system CD. All data will be lost so be sure to have a backup.

Reseat hard drive cable connections, or replace if bad.

If nothing works, Apple recommends replacing the hard drive.

InfraRed remote problems

IrDA problems (only on early iMacs)

Trouble

You can't connect to two infrared-equipped units.

Probable cause

Infrared device has dirt on it.

Incorrect distance between devices and devices are at wrong angle.

IrDA settings not correct.

Devices are not compatible.

Bad IrDA board or cable connections.

Bad IrDA port on the A/V interconnect board.

Possible fix

Clean infrared window.

Devices should be spaced between three and six feet and at angled less than twenty degrees.

Check or set IrDA control panel (select "Auto Connect").

Reseat the IrDA cable that connects the IrDA board to the A/V interconnect board and the IrDA cable that runs between the A/V interconnect board and the logic board, and the IrDA cable that runs between the IrDA board and the audio/video interconnect board.

If nothing works, Apple recommends replacing the logic board, IrDA board, or A/V interconnect board.

Modem problems

Trouble

Your iMac does not recognize the modem.

Probable cause

Internal modem does not work.

Modem not seated properly.

Bad parameter RAM.

Modem files not installed or corrupted.

Possible fix

Reinstall iMac modem extension and the iMac internal modem CCL.

Zap PRAM. Hold down **Command-Option-P-R** keys on startup or use TechTool.

Reseat modem card.

Replace modem.

Modem dialing problems

Trouble

Modem does not dial out.

No dial tone heard.

Modem not found.

iMac freezes when modem dials.

Modem not connecting or drops when it does.

Error launching a Web browser.

Dialup software problem.

Trouble connecting to Net site.

Disconnected after being idle.

Probable cause

Line not plugged into wall jack or modem.

Loose phone line cable.

Bad phone jack.

Phone line dead.

Modem settings incorrect.

Extensions conflict.

TCP/IP control panel not configured correctly.

Net provider is down.

Time out set too short.

Possible fix

Reseat phone line into jack on computer or wall.

Try a phone in the phone line to see if it is dead. Contact phone company if it is.

Reseat the modem card.

Replace the modem card if defective.

Reinstall modem software. Be sure internal 56k modem is selected in the modem control panel.

Troubleshoot extensions. Start with the last one added if you just installed new software.

Reinstall system software.

Reinstall Net Browser software.

Reinstall dialup software.

Check phone line for noise and try another phone jack.

Be sure TCP/IP control panel is configured properly.

Turn off call waiting (in the init string of the dialup application. Use the string *70.).

Check to make sure the TCP/IP control panel is correctly for Net provider.

Net provider may be down. Contact them.

Network problems

Trouble

Cannot switch to Ethernet in the control panel.

No devices visible in Chooser.

Probable cause

Wrong selection in the Network control panel.

Corrupted PRAM.

System software corrupted.

Bad Ethernet cable, hub, or port.

Network is down.

Possible fix

Open the Network control panel and select the Ethernet option. If devices appear, problem is solved.

Zap PRAM. Hold down **Command-Option-P-R** during startup, or use TechTool.

Reinstall system software from CD that came with iMac.

Reseat or replace Ethernet cable.

Examine hub and put cable into different port.

Replace hub.

If nothing works, Apple recommends replacing the logic board.

Peripheral problems

Cursor problems

Trouble

Cursor doesn't move on display.

Clicking on mouse does nothing.

Double clicking on mouse does not open program, disk, or server.

Probable cause

Corrupted parameter RAM.

Bad USB port.

System software corrupted.

Possible fix

Zap RAM. Hold down **Command-Option-P-R** during startup or use TechTool.

Reinstall system software from CD that came with iMac.

Attach device to a different USB port. If it works, the original port is bad.

Replace keyboard or mouse if they are bad.

If nothing works, Apple recommends replacing the logic board.

Printing problems
USB printer problems
Trouble

USB printer does not print.

Probable cause

Bad printer or it is not USB compatible.

Bad printer cable.

Printer drivers corrupted or not installed.

iMac does not have iMac Update installed.

Printer not selected in Chooser.

Bad USB port.

Bad hub (if using one).

Bad system software.

Possible fix

Reinstall printer drivers.

Select printer in Chooser.

Try another printer cable.

Reinstall system software.

Try printer in different USB port to make sure port is good.

If nothing works, try a different printer or if this is a PC printer try a third-party solution like PowerPrint.

Try a different hub.

If nothing works, Apple recommends replacing the logic board.

Networked printer problems

Trouble

Network printer does not print.

Probable cause

Bad network connections.

System software or printer drivers corrupted or wrong version installed.

Printer not selected in Chooser.

Bad printer or cable not seated or bad.

Possible fix

Perform a clean install of the system software from the CD that came with your iMac.

Check network connections for break.

Reseat or replace cable connection from printer to network.

Replace printer.

If nothing works, Apple recommends replacing the logic board.

USB problems

Trouble

System hangs or error box appears.

Probable cause

Early iMacs do not have the latest iMac Update installed.

USB device drivers corrupted or not installed.

Possible fix

Be sure to run the latest version of iMac Update from Apple's Software Upgrade Web (**http://www.apple.com/swupdates**). If you have early iMacs you should run the following updates:

iMac Firmware Update 1.2

iMac Update 1.0

iMac CD Update

iMac Update 1.1

iMac Internal 56k Modem Script

Apple Modem Updater

Apple Ethernet Speed & Duplex Tool 6.2.1a4c1

Apple System Profiler 2.1.2

Mac OS ROM Update 1.0

ATI Video Software Update

USB Mass Storage Support

Epson Stylus Color 740/740i 5.5BE

ColorSync 2.5.1

Apple Memory Guide

Apple Spec Database

Apple/GV 56K Updaters 1.1.3

Mac OS 8.6 Update

Apple Spec Database

OpenGL 1.1.2

Trouble

USB device fails to function from lack of power.

Probable cause

Not enough power from hub or power source of connected peripheral.

USB drivers not installed or corrupted.

Bad USB device or connector.

Possible fix

Reconnect problem device into different USB port to check port or device status.

Replace bad device or port.

Reinstall device drivers.

If nothing works, Apple recomends replacing the logic board.

Video problems

Trouble

Video is unstable or absent.

Rolling horizontal/vertical lines.

Power on.

Probable cause

PRAM corrupted.

Processor module not seated correctly or bad.

SDRAM not seated correctly or bad.

Video or RGB cable not seated or bad.

Bad CRT.

Possible fix

Zap PRAM. Hold down **Command-Option-P-R** during startup or use TechTool.

If you did not hear a normal boot-up chime, when you start the computer reseat the processor module or the SDRAM.

If you didn't hear a normal boot up chime reseat and check the internal RGB cable attached to the A/V interconnect board at location J5, or the internal video cable attached to the logic board at location J16 and the A/V interconnect board at location J2, and the internal RGB cable attached to the video portion of the analog/video board at board at location P301. Reseat or replace them if they are defective.

If nothing works, Apple recommends resetting the Cuda chip or logic board, or replacing the processor module, logic board, analog/video board, A/V inter-connect board, or CRT.

No video

Trouble

Normal startup boot chime.

Green startup LED visible.

Fan is running.

Display is solid gray.

Probable cause

Corrupted PRAM.

System software corrupted.

Internal RGB or video cable not seated.

Bad CRT.

Possible fix

Zap PRAM. Hold down **Command-Option-P-R** during startup or use TechTool.

Reinstall system software from the CD that came with the computer.

Reseat, or replace if bad, the internal RGB cable that attaches to the A/V interconnect board at location J5, or the internal video cable attached to the logic board at location J16 and the A/V interconnect board at location J2.

Reseat or replace if bad the internal video cable attached to the logic board at location J16, the A/V interconnect board at location J2, and the internal RGB cable attached to the A/V interconnect board at location J5 and the video board at location P301.

If nothing works Apple recommends resetting the Cuda chip or logic board, or replacing the analog/video board, the A/V interconnect board, the logic board, or the CRT.

Trouble

Distorted video.

Thin white line.

Probable cause

Display adjustment, screen geometry, screen cutoff or white balance out of adjustment.

Possible fix

Readjust using the monitors control panel.

Trouble

Thin, white horizontal line scrolls from top to bottom, or bottom to top on the display, appearing most often at 1024 x 768 resolution.

Probable cause

Cutoff or white balance needs adjusting.

Analog/video board not seated or defective.

Possible fix

Readjust the cutoff or white balance.

Reseat the analog/video board.

If nothing works, Apple recommends replacing the analog/video board.

Tinting video

Trouble

Display is tinted.

Probable cause

Video or RGB cable not seated properly or defective.

iMac too close to other electrical appliances.

Color balance not correct.

Possible fix

Move iMac to another location away from any other electrical devices.

Reseat or replace the video cable from the interconnect board to the main logic board (behind the CD-ROM drive).

Reseat or replace the internal RGB cable at location J5 on the A/V interconnect board and at location P301 on the analog/video board.

Adjust the white balance.

If nothing works, Apple recommends replacing the analog/video board.

Scrambled or ghost video

Trouble

Text or characters appear on screen that you did not place there.

Probable cause

System software corrupted.

Bad VRAM.

Possible fix

Change the resolution in the Monitors control panel and reboot. If screen is normal, reinstall the system software that came with your computer.

Reseat or replace VRAM DIMMs.

If nothing works, Apple recommends replacing the logic board.

Trouble

Screen goes blank when you are trying to change resolution on the fly to higher 1024 x 768 resolution of Model A iMac (original).

Probable cause
Not enough video RAM (Model A came with 2Mb).

Possible fix
Increase your video RAM to 6Mb.

iBook Troubleshooting

Apple Mac System startup problems

Error beeps

Trouble
One beep is heard when starting up.

Probable cause
No RAM is detected in the iBook.

Possible fix
Reseat RAM if there is any in the iBook.
Install RAM.

Trouble
Two beeps are heard when starting up.

Probable cause
Wrong memory is installed. EDO has been installed instead of SDRAM SODIMMs.

Possible fix
Take out the EDO RAM and install SDRAM SODIMMs.

Trouble
Three beeps are heard when starting up.

Probable cause
None of the RAM banks passed the memory test.

Trouble

Four beeps are heard when starting up.

Probable cause

The ROM is bad.

Possible fix

There isn't any. You have to bring it in.

Trouble

When you start up you get the following dialog box: "Built-in memory test has detected an error."

Probable cause

RAM not seated properly or bad.

Possible fix

Reseat the RAM card, or replace it if bad.

Power problems

Trouble

Computer won't start up.

Probable cause

Bad battery.

Bad power adapter.

Internal keyboard not seated or bad.

Bad RAM or expansion card (AirPort).

Possible fix

Reset the Power Manager. Press the Reset button above the Power button then wait a few seconds and press the Power button.

Try a different power adapter.

Try it without the battery; replace battery if defective.

Disconnect the internal keyboard completely and restart. If iMac works, you need to bring it to Apple repair.

If you added new memory, take it out and try again. If iMac works, replace bad RAM.

Remove the AirPort card if you have it and try to boot up. If yes, replace the card.

If nothing works, you need to schedule an Apple authorized repair.

Trouble
Computer runs when plugged into wall outlet but not on battery power.

Probable cause
Battery not seated properly.

Bad battery.

Possible fix
Power down the computer. Reset the Power Manager by pressing the Reset button above the Power button. Wait a few seconds then press the power button.

Reseat battery. Test with another good battery.

If nothing works, you need to schedule an Apple authorized repair.

Trouble
Computer runs with battery, but not with the power adapter plugged into wall outlet.

Probable cause
Wall outlet power off.

Bad power adapter.

Possible fix
Try another wall outlet.

Try another good power adaptor (be sure lights are on around the power port—green or amber). Replace if original is bad.

Power down the computer. Reset the Power Manager by pressing the Reset button above the Power button. Wait a few seconds then press the power button.

If nothing works, you need to schedule an Apple authorized repair.

Trouble

Screen is blank.

Backlight is off.

No response from iBook.

Probable cause

No power to computer.

Bad battery.

Bad power adapter.

Possible fix

Try another battery or power adapter. Replace if defective.

Reset the computer by holding Command Control, Power button simultaneously.

Power down the computer. Reset the Power Manager by pressing the Reset button above the Power button. Wait a few seconds then press the Power button.

Zap PRAM. Press the Power button, then hold down **Command-Option-P-R** until you hear the startup chime twice.

If you have installed new memory, take it out and try to restart. If it starts, replace bad memory.

Remove keyboard and try to start. Replace keyboard if defective.

If nothing works, you need to schedule an Apple authorized repair.

Trouble

Power adapter is plugged in.

Control strip doesn't indicate adapter is connected.

Probable cause

Power adapter not connected firmly into wall socket or power cord not seated firmly into adapter.

Possible fix

Reseat the power cord and adapter and try again. Replace if cord/adapter is defective.

Try another power outlet.

Power down the computer. Reset the Power Manager by pressing the Reset button above the Power button. Wait a few seconds then press the Power button.

If nothing works, you need to schedule an Apple authorized repair.

Trouble

Battery won't charge.

Probable cause

Bad battery.

Possible fix

Try another good battery to make sure, replace original if defective.

Power down the iBook. Press the Reset button above the Power button and wait a few seconds before you press the Power button.

Take out the battery and reinsert it, leaving it for 15 seconds. Try this several times.

If nothing works, you need to schedule an Apple authorized repair.

Trouble

Battery will not charge unless unit is in sleep mode or shut down.

Probable cause

You are using the wrong power adapter.

Possible fix

Make sure you are using the right power adapter with a 45-watt rating.

If nothing works, you need to schedule an Apple authorized repair.

Audio problems

Trouble

No sound coming from speaker.

Probable cause

Mute selection is on or volume is not up.

External speakers or headphones are plugged in.

Possible fix

Open the Sound control panel and make sure mute is not selected or hit **F6** on the keyboard.

Increase volume by pressing **F4** on the keyboard.

Disconnect any external speakers or headphones and test them.

Zap PRAM. Press the Power button, then hold down **Command-Option-P-R** keys until you hear the startup chime twice, or use Techtool.

If nothing works, you need to schedule an Apple authorized repair.

Trouble

Only the startup sound is heard, then silence.

Probable cause

Corrupted preference file.

Possible fix

Delete the sound preference file found in the Preferences folder in the system folder. Zap PRAM. Press the Power button, then hold down **Command-Option-P-R** until you hear the startup chime twice, or use Techtool.

Reinstall the System software that came with your iBook (do a clean install)

Trouble

Volume control does not operate it should.

Probable cause

Stuck Fn key.

Mute is on.

Sound control panel software is corrupted.

Possible fix

Verify the Fn keys are all right.

Verify that the Monitors & Sound control panel settings are correct.

Turn mute mode off if it is on.

In the Keyboard control panel be sure that "hot keys" is enabled.

Reset the Power Manager. Press the Reset button above the Power button. Wait a few seconds before you press the Power button.

If nothing works, you need to schedule an Apple authorized repair.

CD-ROM drive problems

Trouble

Drive does not accept disc (mechanical failure).

Probable cause

Disc not seated properly.

Possible fix

Take out disc and reinsert making sure it is properly seated.

If that does not work, you need to schedule an Apple authorized repair.

Trouble

Disc icon does not show up on desktop, or dialog box appears, wanting to initialize disc.

Probable cause

Not a CD disc. Is it a DVD?

CD software drivers not installed or corrupted.

Possible fix

Try a different CD-only disc.

Clean disc.

Reinstall CD drivers.

If nothing works, you need to schedule an Apple authorized repair.

Hard drive problems

Trouble

Internal hard drive does not spin.

Probable cause

No power to hard drive.

Power adapter is not seated correctly.

USB driver conflict.

Hard drive cables not seated properly.

Bad hard drive.

Possible fix

Reseat power adapter.

Disconnect any USB devices connected to the iBook and test.

Use Drive Setup utility to verify that the hard drive is recognized.

Reseat hard drive cables.

Replace hard drive.

If nothing works, you need to schedule an Apple authorized repair.

Trouble

Hard drive is slow to respond, or screen goes blank too often.

Probable cause

Energy Saver control panel settings not correct.

Possible fix

Open the Energy Saver control panel and adjust the sleep delay.

Connect power adapter.

Miscellaneous problems

Trouble

Sleep light won't come on.

Probable cause

iBook is not in sleep mode.

Possible fix

Turn it on.

Reset the power manager. Press the reset button above the Power button. Wait a few seconds before you press the Power button.

If nothing works, you need to schedule and Apple authorized repair.

Trouble

Screen goes blank and computer shuts down every few minutes.

Probable cause

Sleep delay set wrong.

Power adapter faulty, or wrong one being used.

Possible fix

In the Energy Saver control panel, change the settings.

Reseat the power adapter. Replace if defective.

Trouble

Software application seems to run slower after a few seconds.

Probable cause

Wrong setting in the Energy Saver control panel.

Possible fix

Turn off "Allow Processor Cycling" in the Energy Save control panel.

If this does not work, you need to schedule an Apple authorized repair.

Modem problems

Trouble

No dial tone detected.

Probable cause

Phone line dead.

Phone cable is not seated properly in wall or in iBook.

Cable is plugged into Ethernet port, not the modem port (they are different sizes).

Bad modem.

Possible fix

Try another phone line.

Inspect the modem port to make sure the line is plugged in correctly.

Reseat the phone cable in both wall and iBook.

Apple says that if you are using Apple Remote Access 3.0, try selecting the "Ignore Dial Tone" in the Modem control panel. If it connects, try another phone line. If using a third-party communications program, enter **atx1** to disable tone detection. You can reset the modem back to the factory settings by entering the **atz** command during a session.

Replace modem.

If nothing works, you need to schedule an Apple authorized repair.

Trouble

No internal modem selection available.

Probable cause

Modem software not installed or corrupted.

Possible fix

Reinstall modem software.

Zap PRAM. Press the Power button, then hold down **Command-Option-P-R** until you hear the startup chime twice, or use Techtool.

Reinstall system software with the CD that came with your iBook (do a clean install).

If nothing works, you need to schedule an Apple authorized repair.

Printing problems

Trouble

Ethernet network printer does not print.

Probable cause

Printer is not selected in Chooser.

Printer drivers not installed or corrupted.

Cables not seated properly or bad.

Possible fix

Select the printer in Chooser.

Reinstall the printer drivers.

Zap PRAM. Press the Power button, then hold down the **Command-Option-P-R** keys until you hear the startup chime twice, or use Techtool.

Reseat all cables

Attach computer directly to printer using Ethernet crossover cable (Belkin has them—**www.belkin. com**), and retest.

If nothing works, you need to schedule an Apple authorized repair.

Trouble

USB printer does not print.

Probable cause

Printer drivers are not installed or corrupted.

Printer not selected in Chooser.

USB cables not seated firmly or bad.

Possible fix

Reinstall printer drivers.

Reseat USB cable or replace if defective.

Zap PRAM. Press the Power button, then hold down the **Command-Option-P-R** keys until you hear the startup chime twice, or use TechTool.

Open the Chooser and make sure the printer is selected.

Verify that the printer is recognized by the computer by opening the Apple System Profiler in the Apple menu.

If nothing works, you need to schedule an Apple authorized repair.

USB peripheral problems

Trouble

After you connect external USB device, computer does not start up.

Probable cause

USB driver is not correct or corrupted.

USB peripheral bad.

USB cables not seated properly or bad.

Possible fix

Reinstall USB device driver and make sure it is the latest version.

After disconnecting all devices, plug them in one at a time to eliminate the problem one.

Turn on external USB device first if it is self powered.

Reseat all USB cables or replace the one that is found to be defective.

If nothing works, you need to schedule an Apple authorized repair.

Trouble

USB device not recognized by computer.

Probable cause

USB driver for device is not installed or corrupted.

Bad USB port.

Bad USB device.

Extension conflict.

Possible fix

Reinstall device drivers.

If it is a digital camera, begin the downloading command before you turn on the camera.

Try another USB peripheral on the same port to see if the port is bad.

Unplug all USB peripherals and reconnect one at a time to find the culprit.

If using a USB/serial adapter, verify that it is compatible with the iBook and your system software version.

Reinstall system software with clean install.

Troubleshoot extensions.

If nothing works, you need to schedule an Apple authorized repair.

Trouble

I/O devices are unrecognized, or garbage is transmitted or received.

Probable cause

USB device cables are not seated properly or bad.

USB Device drivers not installed or corrupted.

Extension conflict.

Possible fix

Reseat all USB cables, replace defective one if found.

Reinstall USB device drivers making sure they are the latest versions and compatible with the version of the system software you are using.

Troubleshoot extensions.

Reinstall system software performing a clean install.

If nothing works, you need to schedule an Apple authorized repair.

Trouble

USB printer does not print.

Probable cause

Printer drivers are not installed or corrupted.

Printer not selected in Chooser.

USB cables not seated firmly or bad.

Possible fix

Reinstall printer drivers.

Reseat USB cable or replace if defective.

Zap PRAM. Press the Power button, then hold down **Command-Option-P-R** keys until you hear the startup chime twice, or use TechTool.

Open the Chooser and make sure the printer is selected.

Verify that the printer is recognized by the computer by opening the Apple System Profiler in the Apple menu.

If nothing works, you need to schedule an Apple authorized repair.

Trouble

USB device experiences a partial lack of power.

USB device doesn't have enough power to function.

Probable cause

Power cord not seated properly or defective.

Possible fix

Plug the USB device into another electrical device if it is independently powered.

Plug it into a HUB or another device already powered, provided it has a receptacle.

Trouble

After sleep, a USB peripheral is sometimes not recognized.

Probable cause

Device driver corrupted or wrong version.

Possible fix

Reinstall the latest drivers from the manufacturer.

Restart the iBook.

If nothing works, you need to schedule an Apple authorized repair.

Keyboard and trackpad problems

Trouble

No response from any key on keyboard.

Probable cause

iBook is not turned on.

System software corrupted.

Possible fix

Be sure the iBook is powered up.

Reset the Power Manager. Press the Reset button above the Power button. Wait a few seconds before you press the Power button.

Power up the iBook using your system software CD. If it works, then reinstall the system software.

Reseat the keyboard cable.

If nothing works, you need to schedule an Apple authorized repair.

Trouble

Cursor does not move when you are using trackpad.

Probable cause

Another USB device is conflicting.

Trackpad connection is not seated properly on logic board.

Possible fix

Remove any other USB device and test.

Reset the Power Manager. Press the Reset button above the Power button. Wait a few seconds before you press the Power button.

Take off the RAM access door and reseat the trackpad connection to the logic board.

If nothing works, you need to schedule and Apple authorized repair.

Trouble

Cursor moves on screen with external mouse connected, but clicking or double clicking the mouse has no effect.

Probable cause

Keyboard USB port is faulty.

Bad or dirty mouse.

Possible fix

Connect the mouse to the iBook USB port.

Clean the mouse.

Power up the iBook with your system software to verify it isn't software problem. If it is, perform a clean install.

Trouble

Cursor moves, but clicking trackpad button has no effect.

Probable cause

Charging board is not connected to the logic board.

Top case not seated properly.

Possible fix

Reset the Power Manager. Press the reset button above the Power button. Wait a few seconds before you press the Power button.

Press trackpad button on charging board with a non-metal object. If button activates cursor, check top case seating.

Check to see if the charging board is connected to the logic board.

If nothing works, Apple recommends replacing the charging board or Trackpad button actuator that is on the top case.

Trouble

Cursor does not move on the screen with an external mouse, but USB external keyboard works.

Probable cause

Mouse not secured firmly.

Mouse is dirty.

Corrupted system software.

Possible fix

Try another mouse in same situation to see if mouse is bad; replace if it is.

Reseat the mouse in the port.

Clean the mouse.

If cursor works after booting from your system software CD, reinstall the system software using a clean install.

Try connecting mouse to another port.

Replace mouse.

If nothing works, you need to schedule an Apple authorized repair.

Trouble

Cursor intermittently does not move or moves erratically.

Probable cause

Dirty trackpad.

Trackpad connection logic board faulty.

Corrupted system software.

Possible fix

Reset the Power Manager. Press the Reset button above the Power button. Wait a few seconds before you press the Power button.

If using power adapter, try battery power. Replace adapter if faulty.

Be sure you are only using one finger at a time on the trackpad.

Clean the trackpad surface with a material that will not create static electricity.

Power up from system software CD. If problem is corrected, reinstall fresh system software.

Insure that the trackpad connection is firm on the logic board.

If nothing works, you need to schedule an Apple authorized repair.

Video problems

Trouble

Partial or full row of pixels is always on or never comes on.

Multiple vertical or horizontal rows of pixels are always on or never come on.

Probable cause

Bad display. (One or two bad pixels in an LCD display are normal, however).

Possible fix

Nothing; you need to schedule an Apple authorized repair.

Trouble

No display, but computer appears to operate correctly.

Probable cause

Screen brightness adjustment not correct.

Battery drained.

Possible fix

Connect the power adapter.

Increase screen brightness setting with **Fn** key pressed or not pressed.

Restart computer by holding **Command-Control-Power** button.

Power down the iBook. Press the Reset button above the Power button and wait a few seconds before you press the Power button.

If nothing works, you need to schedule an Apple authorized repair.

Trouble

Backlight is off.

Screen is very dim.

Probable cause

Screen brightness setting is incorrect.

Possible fix

Readjust the screen brightness setting.

If that does not work, you need to schedule an Apple authorized repair.

Trouble

Display is very light or totally white.

Probable cause

Display cable and inverter board cable connections not seated properly or defective.

Possible fix

Reinstall system software to see if it is a software problem.

Reseat the display cable and inverter board cable connections on the logic board. Replace them if they are defective.

If nothing works, you need to schedule an Apple authorized repair.

Using the Net for Help!

The Internet

The Internet, or the "Net," is a worldwide computer network comprised of millions of people and billions of pieces of information all accessible at the click of your mouse.

Thirty years after it was created by the U.S. Army, as a defense network, the now public Internet has more than 36 million host computers, in more than 170 countries. It is estimated that more 170 million people use the Internet.

There are several Internet tools: e-mail discussion lists, Usenet newsgroups, and the Web, that can help you obtain information on upgrading, troubleshooting, and repairing your G3 Mac. This chapter shows you how to use them.

Internet Mailing (Discussion) Lists

An Internet Mailing or Discussion List is an electronic equivalent of a board meeting, conference call, or user group meeting. It allows you to correspond with other online users anywhere in the world. The difference is, you can discuss your topic 24 hours a day 7 days a week and you don't have to be in a room at a set time. It all takes place over the Net through your e-mail account.

There are several different kinds of mailing lists used to share information. Mailing lists that are designed as a one-way broadcast are called *Automailers*, or *Announcement* lists. You receive them, but are not allowed to reply. They are primarily used to respond to a specific request like a news or software update, a new product introduction, or instructions on downloading software.

Some mailing lists contain information as organized articles, tips, tutorials, news; these are more technically known as electronic newsletters. While most are sent as plain text e-mails, there are more elaborate ones produced with special software programs that allow the publisher to include layouts with beautiful color covers and graphics just like a printed newsletter or magazine counterpart.

The majority of the mailing lists featured here are multi-way electronic discussions. They are free to all to join and discuss all aspects of your Macintosh computer.

To participate in a mailing list you must subscribe to it. You subscribe by using your e-mail account and it takes only minutes. Send an e-mail to a specific address, called the administrative address, and in the subject line, or body of the e-mail, enter a command, usually "subscribe *name of the list*" and your name or e-mail address. On some, you don't need to place your name, just the name of the list. On other lists you send an e-mail to the address and the list software uses your e-mail address automatically as the subscription address. Some list maintainers send you an e-mail that you must reply to in order to activate the subscription. This ensures that you really want to join the list, and proves to the list maintainer you are real and that the address is reachable. Finally, some list maintainers, as in *moderated lists*, have to approve your subscription request. This approval is not automatic.

There are two addresses associated with a mailing list. When you post to the list you do not use the one you used for subscribing, the *administrative address*. There is always a second address to send an actual posting. Be sure to read the confirming e-mail that comes back to you after you subscribe to a list. It describes the rules and functions for the list.

There are many Internet mailing lists and electronic newsletters that deal with all models of the Macintosh, although our focus is the G3 models, as well as software, peripheral hardware, development, the computer industry in general, and other issues relating to the Mac.

Many of the lists are for general, non-technical users and there are lists for the new user, the technically inclined, and software or hardware topics. You can gain a great deal of technical help from fellow Mac users through these discussion lists.

Mailing lists usually come in two versions, individual and *digest*. If there is a digest version available, it's wise to subscribe to it instead of the individual list, especially if it's a very active list. You may find your mailbox overflowing with e-mail if the list is popular. Some lists generate hundreds of e-mails a day. A digest sends only one file to your mailbox with all the day's or week's posting. You download the file and read it when you have time.

While most mailing lists are open to all, there are some that are "moderated." A moderated list is controlled by the list maintainer, who has complete control over what gets posted. You send the moderator your posting and he or she determines if it is suitable for the list. Moderated lists tend to be more focused and on subject than the free-flowing non-moderated lists.

It is important to understand the rules of the list. Once you subscribe, you'll receive an e-mail with instructions on how to unsubscribe, as well as search the archives, if archives are maintained, and other administrative functions. Keep that e-mail in a place where you can find it easily. You will need it when you want to get off the list but can't remember how.

All the mailing lists described below are available to you free. A short summary of their purpose, taken from the original sources, and instructions for subscribing are included. Be sure to check Apple's Web site for any new mailing lists at **http://www.lists.apple.com/**.

G3 Specific Lists

iBook users

Here is a list specifically for Apple's new iBook and its users.

You can subscribe by sending e-mail to:

- **iBook-ON@themacintoshguy.com** and including your e-mail address, or
- **iBook-DIGEST@themacintoshguy.com** to subscribe to the digest version.

iMac update

iMac Update is published by Apple Computer. Go to the iMac web site at: **http://www.apple.com/imac/imac99/index.html**.

You can subscribe to iMac Update there.

MacFireWireTalk

Here is a list where you can discuss the use of FireWire and FireWire peripherals. Send a message to **macjordomo@themacintoshguy.com** and in the body of the message include: *subscribe MacFireWireTalk Your_Name.*

Macintosh USB Talk List

Here is a list where you can discuss the Universal Serial Bus (USB) and its use. To subscribe send a message to: **macjordomo@themacintoshguy.com**. In the body of the message include: *subscribe MacUSBTalk Your Name*.

Sherlock-Talk

Here is a list where you can discuss all areas of writing Sherlock Plug-ins. To subscribe, send e-mail to: **requests@lists.mdg.com** and in the subject heading include: *Subscribe Sherlock-Talk*.

To subscribe to the digest version, include: *Subscribe Digest Sherlock-Talk*.

The iMac List Digest

This is an e-mail mailing list developed for iMac users sponsored by NoBeige.com. You can subscribe by going to the NoBeige.com Web site at: **http://www.nobeige. com/**.

The iMac List

This is for general discussion about the iMac. To subscribe, send e-mail to: **get-imac@reformed.net**. The list server will use your return address as your subscription address.

Other Useful Mailing Lists

Apple eNews

Apple eNews is a newsletter published by Apple Computer that informs you about new developments, products, and news about Apple. It's published twice a month. You can subscribe to the newsletter by going to the following web site: **http://www.apple.com/ hotnews/subscribe.html**.

More information about the list can be found at: **http://www.lists.apple.com/applewire.html**.

Apple press releases

This list will send you Apple's press releases as they are issued. Subscribe by going to: **http://support. info.apple.com/support/supportoptions/lists.html** or send e-mail to: **pressrel@thing2.info.apple.com** and in the Subject heading type: *subscribe pressrel*.

Apple software update locations

This list will send you Apple's software locations once. Subscribe as needed by going to: **http://support.info. apple.com/support/supportoptions/lists.html**.

Apple-Net-Announce

This list is moderated and is the posting of announcements and press releases involving products related to Apple computers and Inter/intranets. To subscribe, send e-mail to: **majordomo@public.lists.apple.com** and include in the body the line: *subscribe Apple-Net-Announce*.

Apple-Workgroup-Servers

Here is a discussion list for those who use or administer Workgroup Servers. To subscribe, send e-mail to: **majordomo@public. lists.apple.com** and in the body of the message, include: *subscribe Apple-Workgroup-Servers*.

To subscribe to the digest versions, in the body, include: *subscribe Apple-Workgroup-Servers-digest*.

Archive site

This is a list that lets you know about software updates. To subscribe, send e-mail to: **Majordomo@**

cc.rochester.edu and in the body of the message, include: *subscribe archive_site*.

eMac Daily

eMac Daily is a daily news service for the Macintosh community that provides late-breaking industry news about new product announcements, new software, updates, and special deals. This list is being produced by MacDirectory in conjunction with MacCentral (both sites are describe later in this chapter). Subscribe by sending an e-mail to: **eMac-Daily@macdirectory.com** and in the subject of the message type: *SUBSCRIBE*.

Future Apple Systems technologies

According to Apple, this list is for discussing future Apple technologies like revisions of the Mac OS operating system, QuickTime upgrades, new logic boards, cache designs, and the like. To subscribe, send e-mail to: **lyris@clio.lyris.net**. Include in the body of the message: *subscribe fast Your Name*.

Info-MAC

Info-Mac is the oldest Macintosh discussion list. It is only available as a digest and is moderated. To subscribe, send e-mail to: **info-mac@starnine.com**. Include in the subject line: *subscribe*.

Mac-Chat

Mac Chat is a spinoff from the Mac-L list. This is for those members who tend to take discussions a bit off-track from those being discussed in the Mac-L list. To subscribe, send e-mail to: **lyris@clio.lyris.net** and in the body of the text, include: *subscribe Mac-Chat your_name*.

MACHRDWR

This moderated list is for posting of alerts about hardware problems and repairs for Macintosh equipment and peripherals from other vendors.

To subscribe, send e-mail to: **listserv@LISTSERV. DARTMOUTH. EDU** and in the body of the message, include: *subscribe machrdwr Your Name*.

macissues

This list is for discussing all Mac related issues. To subscribe send e-mail to: **listproc@listproc. bgsu.edu**. In the body of the e-mail, include: *subscribe macissues YOUR FULL NAME*.

Mac-L

This list includes discussions in technical issues for the average and advanced user involving the MacOS and related hardware issues. To subscribe, send e-mail to: **lyris@clio.lyris.net**. In the body of the message, include: *subscribe Mac-L yourfirstname yourlastname*.

MacTalk

This is a list for more complex problems. New users are discouraged. It is hosted by Radix Consulting Ltd., a Macintosh-oriented computer consulting firm specializing in database design and internet connectivity. Subscribe by going to: **http://www.r8ix.com/ lists.html** or send e-mail to: **majordomo@r8ix.com**. Include in the body of the message: *subscribe MacTalk yourrealname*.

MacMarines MailCall

MacMarines is a moderated list about Mac issues. To subscribe, send e-mail to: **Requests@MacMarines. com**. In the body of your message put: *Subscribe Mailcall* or *Subscribe Digest Mailcall*.

MacMarines also has a web site at **http://www. macmarines.com/**.

MACSYSTM

This list is for discussion of the Mac system software and everything that deals with it, like INITS and Control Panels. To subscribe, send e-mail to: **LISTSERV@ LISTSERV.DARTMOUTH.EDU** and in the body of the e-mail, include: *SUBSCRIBE MACSYSTM*.

Mac Virus

This is a list that announces viruses on the Mac. To subscribe, send e-mail to: **listproc@listproc.bgsu. edu**. In the body of the message, type: *subscribe mac-virus-announce YOUR FULL NAME*.

Powerbooks

This is a list to discuss Powerbooks and other Mac portables. To subscribe, send e-mail to: **lists@ reformed.net.** Include in the body of the message: *subscribe Powerbooks Your Name* [name is optional].

To subscribe to a daily digest send e-mail to: **lists@reformed.net**. Include in the body of the message: *set Powerbooks digest*.

Power Macintosh Bulletin

This is a special mailing from Apple devoted to the Power Macintosh. It notifies you of the latest product news and information, as well as changes to the Power Macintosh Web site. To subscribe, send e-mail to: **requests@thing1. info.apple.com**. Include in the subject line: *subscribe powermacintosh*.

Powermacs

This is a list for users of PowerPC-based Macintoshes. To subscribe, send e-mail to: **lists@reformed.net**.

Include in the body of the message: *subscribe PowerMacs Your Name* [name is optional].

To subscribe to a daily digest, send e-mail to: **lists@reformed.net**. Include in the body of the message: *set PowerMacs digest.*

The Information Alley

This compilation of new and updated Tech Info Library articles is sent daily by service and support engineers and writers. To subscribe send e-mail to: **listproc@ listproc.info.apple.com**. Include in the body of the message: *subscribe infoalley* (and your name).

TidBITS

TidBITS is an excellent Mac electronic newsletter/list. To subscribe, send e-mail to: **tidbits-on@tidbits.com**. No special subject or body is necessary.

Finding More Mailing Lists

New mailing lists are being created every day. You can find them easily by visiting a few Web sites devoted to maintaining a complete list of mailing lists.

Apple Web site

http://www.lists.apple.com/
This address will take you right to Apple's list of available Apple-related mailing lists. Check here first for any new lists.

Publicly accessible mailing lists

http://www.neosoft.com/internet/paml/
This is the oldest list of lists on the Net and started in 1981. It is one of the more reliable search engines. Just type in your keyword or go to the alphabetical or category index.

The search results gives you contact address, summary of the list, how to subscribe or unsubscribe, what listserver software is used, Web address if there is one, a list of keywords used for categorizing the list, and the last time information was updated.

ListsNet

http://www.listsnet.com/

This site groups mailing lists by categories and lets you search by keyword for a particular list. Other features of the site include a hot pick and an e-mail alert feature that will let you know when a new list is added or deleted in the database.

The resulting search gives you a great deal of information including: contact address, summary of list, how to subscribe and unsubscribe, which listserv software and version is used, Web address if there is one, and other categories that might be similar in nature, name of the sponsoring organization, and even the routing address that appears in a list mailing.

Liszt: the mailing list directory

http://www.liszt.com/

This database contains more than 90,000 mailing lists. It is searchable by keyword or categories (and with the ability to filter out junk), or advanced methods. Liszt also has gateways to other search engines so if you don't find what you're looking for, you can easily search a few other search engines automatically. You can submit a list if you like.

The resulting search will list the number of hits by categories. Each list contains the "info" file on the purpose of the list, if it has one. You can also request the "info" file by e-mail, and finally there are instructions on how to subscribe (you can do it from Liszt) or unsubscribe.

Usenet Discussions (Net News)

Another avenue for getting technical help is by participating in Usenet, a global electronic bulletin board for online users. Usenet is a distributed news service that is a collection of public conferences, or discussion groups, called *newsgroups*. You can join and discuss thousands of different topics. Each day millions of people discuss, debate, and share their ideas, opinions, and information. Usenet has no geographic boundaries and it operates 24 hours a day, 7 days a week. It is called "netnews," or "the news," and there are more than 80,000 newsgroups covering every imaginable subject.

There are a couple of ways to get news from Usenet. Chances are your Internet Provider has a Usenet feed and you can grab it locally. Or you can use some of the Web services like DejaNews described later.

You need two things: a client or reader application, called a *newsreader*, and the ability to subscribe to newsgroups.

Subscribing to a newsgroup takes seconds. To subscribe you must have a newsreader. The most convenient newsreader is actually part of Microsoft's Outlook Express e-mail program, but there are many standalone newsreader programs.

A newsreader does all the menial work and lets you read and reply to your favorite newsgroups. A newsreader is used to subscribe and unsubscribe to newsgroups, to read, post, and reply, ignore, and keep track of articles you have read. Newsreaders can keep track of hundreds of messages in hundreds of different newsgroups at the same time, and they make the news easy to read. Newsgroups listed below can provide help for you in fixing and upgrading your G3.

Getting the FAQs

Thousands of new users are entering the Usenet community every day, often asking the same questions.

The newsgroup creator, or one or more regular users of the newsgroup will attempt to alleviate this by collecting all the frequently asked questions, answers, comments, main points, or even a summary of the main elements of discussion in the newsgroup. They create a document called a FAQ (Frequently Asked Questions, pronounced "fack"). Sometimes a FAQ is not really a set of answers to any questions, but more a complete tutorial on the workings of the newsgroup.

The FAQ is usually posted in the newsgroup once a month, even if there are no changes in it. The intention is for new folks to read it. The FAQ for each newsgroup is almost always posted in the news.answers newsgroups, which is the official repository of FAQs.

Before you subscribe or participate in a newsgroup that interests you, read the FAQ if it has one. Make sure you know the purpose of the newsgroup. You will find the FAQs excellent sources of information.

For more information about Usenet in general you can read the following FAQs:

- *A Primer on How to Work with the Usenet Community*, by Chuq Von Rospach
- *FAQs about FAQs*, by Russ Hersch
- *Emily Postnews Answers Your Questions on Netiquette*, by Brad Templeton
- *Hints on Writing Style for Usenet*, by A. Jeff Offutt VI
- *How to Find the Right Place to Post (FAQ)*, by Aliza R. Panitz
- *List of Moderators for Usenet*, by David Lawrence
- *Rules for Posting to Usenet*, by Mark Horton
- *Usenet Software: History and Sources*, by Gene Spafford
- *Usenet FAQ*, by Jerry Schwarz
- *Welcome to news.newusers.questions!* (weekly posting), by Leanne Phillips

- *What is Usenet*, by Chip Salzenberg
- *What is Usenet? A second opinion*, by Edward Vielmetti

You will find these FAQs posted periodically in the news.answers newsgroup. You can read some of these guides online at **http://www.glink.net.hk/GuideTo Usenet.html**.

Mac-related Usenet newsgroups

You can subscribe to any or all of these Mac-related newsgroups using your copy of Outlook Express or any newsreader.

- **alt.mac.updates** (Macintosh software and hardware updates)
- **alt.sys.mac.newuser-help** (a forum for Macintosh users new to the internet)
- **asu.sys.mac** (talk about Macintoshes)
- **biz.marketplace.computers.mac** (Macintosh hardware/software)
- **comp.sys.mac.announce** (important notices for Macintosh users—moderated)
- **comp.sys.mac.hardware** (Macintosh hardware issues and discussions)
- **comp.sys.mac.misc** (general discussions about the Mac—FAQ)
- **comp.sys.mac.portables** (discussion about laptop Macs)
- **comp.sys.mac.system** (discussions of Macintosh system software—FAQ)
- **comp.sys.powerpc** (general PowerPC discussion)
- **misc.forsale.computers.mac-specific.cards. misc** (Macintosh expansion cards)

- **misc.forsale.computers.mac-specific.cards.
  video** (Macintosh video cards)

- **misc.forsale.computers.mac-specific.misc**
  (other Macintosh equipment)

- **misc.forsale.computers.mac-specific.portables**
  (portable Macintosh systems)

- **misc.forsale.computers.mac-specific.software**
  (Macintosh software)

- **misc.forsale.computers.mac-specific.systems**
  (complete Macintosh systems)

Several of the FAQs for these newsgroups can be read
at: **http://www.cis.ohio-state.edu/hypertext/faq/
usenet/**.

Participating in Usenet from the Web

As we mentioned above you can participate in Usenet
even if you don't have a newsreader. With your Web
browser and Net connection, you have access to all the
newsgroups by clicking your mouse. The following
Usenet Web sites will give you access.

Deja.com

(http://www.dejan.com/)
Formerly DejaNews, this is a complete Usenet search
engine that lets you do keyword searches throughout
its Usenet database. You can fine-tune your search by
number of hits or format, sort by date, author, etc.,
and use Boolean search limits OR and AND. You can
also search using an age bias for old or new postings.

The software searches your keywords and gives you
a listing with dates, header info, which newsgroup it
is in, and who posted it. Click on the title and read the
posting. You can even reply or post to the subject if
you want to.

DejaNews allows you gather a profile of any user so be careful where you post and what you post.

The new, redesigned Deja.com is confusing. I like the old design better.

Liszt newsgroups

(http://www.liszt.com/cgi-bin/news.cgi)
This is another very good Usenet search engine. Type in a keyword and it scans the complete 80,000+ newsgroup database and returns a list. You need a Newsgroup server to be able to access them though.

Web Tech Support

The following Web sites cover almost any technical problem, question, or issue that you can think of relating to the Macintosh G3 platform. All these sites provide information at no charge and many are run by dedicated Mac users. The first place to start is Apple's own support page where the company offers technical briefs, tutorials, and articles on all their products.

Apple basic troubleshooting

http://www.info.apple.com/te/troubleshooting/
This Apple site gives you a tutorial on basic Mac troubleshooting.

Apple care support site index

http://www.info.apple.com/siteindex.taf
Start here. This is Apple's index of all support pages for its products.

Apple spec database index

http://www.info.apple.com/info.apple.com/
applespec/applespec.taf
Start here to find spec information on your G3 computer.

Apple tech info library

http://til.info.apple.com/
Apple's technical information library contains more than 15,000 articles covering all aspects of the Mac platform from the latest product information to tech specifications and the latest troubleshooting information or updates. Updated daily, the site contains a search engine to find previously posted material. A section called "Did You Know" highlights information that Apple deems important and current.

Apple tech exchange

http://support.info.apple.com/te/te.taf
This Apple site contains information collected from Apple's Tech Info Library, the software updates archives, discussion forums, and news. There are several categories to choose from, including a special iMac section. Basic troubleshooting, prevention, repair, and common problems are featured.

Extension overload

www.mir.com.my/~cmteng
Extension Overload, created by Teng Chou Ming, is a document with much of information about all the system extensions and control panels inside the System folder of every Macintosh. It lists them by name and explains what they do. Extension Overload also contains information about Mac error codes (now you can know what they mean), Easter Eggs (little surprises hidden somewhere in the software), and other useful things.

Extension Overload v3 covers Extensions and Control Panel from System 7, 7.5, 7.6, Mac OS 8, 8.1, 8.5 and iMac. Currently Extension Overload reviews 756 extensions and 285 control panels. You can subscribe to a newsletter that will inform you of the latest update of Extension Overload.

Experts exchange

http://www.experts-exchange.com/

Experts Exchange offers free answers by technology experts in over 80 computer technology categories. There are categories for Mac networking, applications, communications, and system OS. The site is basically a bulletin board where you post questions and read answers.

Focus on Mac hardware

http://machardware.miningco.com/compute/machardware/

This Web site has many links to hardware-related sites in several categories from classic Macs to video cards. Real-time chats occur and you can read past transcripts. Features and tips are also part of the offerings.

Focus on Mac Support

http://macsupport.miningco.com/compute/macsupport/

This site links to many sites that specialize in Mac support issues from battery issues to virus checkers. Features and tips and chat are also part of the site on Tuesday and Thursday evenings from 8:00-11:00 P.M.

Focus on Mac OS

http://macos.miningco.com/compute/macos/

This site covers the Mac operating system and contains links to OS issues including other operating systems that run on the Mac, like Be or Linux. Features and tips and chat are also part of the site.

iMac2Day

http://www.imac2day.com

iMac2Day features daily news, message boards for discussion, a place to track pricing and availability, a listing of iMac compatible peripherals, reviews, and a great tech support page.

iMac Support Center

http://macsupport.miningco.com/compute/ macsupport/blcenter.htm
There are lots of links to help sites, FAQs, and answers to your questions about anything iMac related. News and features are also on the site.

InformINIT

http://mc04.equinox.net/informinit/
InformINIT is a standalone application which provides information on just about every system folder file there is, such as control panels, extensions, and more.

Internal Apple Codenames

http://www.appleinsider.com/codenames. shtml#desktops
This page lists the various codenames for all Macs.

MacFixIt

http://www.macfixit.com/
This is a great site to visit daily to find out what problems and their fixes are occurring in the Mac world. There is an iMac section that includes troubleshooting, workarounds, and news. If you missed anything, you can search their archives. There is a Sherlock Plug-in for MacFixIt.

MacAnswers

http://www.macanswers.com
This site provides free e-mail tech support. Send them a question via e-mail (**answers@macanswers.com**) and you will get a reply via e-mail within 48 hours.

MacInGuide

http://erols.macinguide.com/technical/index.html
This Web page contains useful information for troubleshooting modem and network setup problems, including dozens of modem initialization strings, system crashes, Internet client software and helpers, and a great guide on how to set up preferences correctly in FreePPP, MacTCP, and TCP/IP so you can get on the Net. Much of the info is geared towards their own service but the information can be applied anywhere.

Macintosh battery page

http://www.academ.com/info/macintosh/
Sometimes when your Mac does not want to start, it's because of a dead battery on the logic board. This page describes how to troubleshoot battery problems, including where to buy batteries.

Macintosh error codes

http://www.cs.cmu.edu/afs/cs/user/lenzo/html/ mac_errors.html
Want to know what error 1010 and hundreds of other system errors mean? This page lists a few hundred of them.

Macintosh parts database

http://machost.blacknight.co.uk/parts.html
This is a great searchable database that gives you the part number for all versions of the Mac and peripherals.

MacintoshOS.com

http://www.macintoshos.com/
This site is a good reference site for system 8 and beyond. Learn tips and shortcuts on using system 8, read news, and find out about updates.

MacInTouch

http://www.macintouch.com/
Ric Ford has been writing about the technical issues of the Macintosh since the beginning. MacInTouch is a daily stop to find out the latest hardware or software problems, upgrades, software updates, and general Apple news. There is a special iMacInTouch section that also produces daily iMac information.

Mac pruning pages

http://cafe.AmbrosiaSW.com/DEF/index.html
This is a good information site if you want to know what a particular control panel or extension does. Dan Frakes, who runs this site, is the author of InformINIT (**http://cafe.AmbrosiaSW.com/DEF/InformINIT. html**), a great database of information on system INITS primarily, but also system folder contents, control panels, and other system-related files.

MacVirus

http://www.macvirus.com/
MacVirus is the one site to visit to learn all about Mac viruses. You can find answers to the most commonly asked virus questions including how to prevent an infection. There are current news and warnings, a complete reference area, and, best of all, an archive of the best virus killer software that you can download.

MacWizard

http://www.interactivepages.com/macfreak/ index1.html
This site is a collection of questions and answers regarding a variety of Mac problems.

No Wonder! Internet technical assistance center

http://www.nowonder.com/
This site has over 350 volunteers from around the world giving free technical support to anyone who asks for it.

Ask a question and get an answer within 24-28 hours. Join their message boards, or participate in live chat if you want to discuss any tech issue with others.

The complete conflict compendium

http://www.mac-conflicts.com/
Interested in all the possible conflicts that can happen to your iMac? You can download them from this site, or visit frequently and read them online. According to the Web site, the Complete Conflict Compendium is a "collection of things that will crash your Mac, or make it act strange." They tell you how to correct it. They cover all Mac operating systems including the early ones and include a special section on the iMac. You can subscribe to a free weekly mailing list and stay on top of possible conflicts.

The G3 all-in-one stop shop

http://members.aol.com/_ht_a/G3AIOGuy/
Here is a great site dedicated to Apple's All In One education machine. News, technical info, a FAQ, guide to software, and links to other sites round out this site maintained by Tom McKenna.

theiMac.com

http://www.theiMac.com/
You can find here features, daily news, columns and tutorials. A weekly live chat, on Tuesdays at 12 P.M. CST and Thursdays at 7PM CST, let you ask ques-

tions, discuss pressing issues, and have fun. Special beginners' guides, upgrade tutorials, software updates, and technical support are also part of the site.

The Mac conflict solution site

http://www.quillserv.com/www/c3/c3.html
Here is a site devoted to solving Mac conflicts especially system extension problems. Each conflict is listed by software, symptoms, how to isolate it and what to do to solve it. This includes problems with Mac's OS 8. A special Help Zone lets you ask questions about a possible conflict occurring in applications, the System, or other Mac area. Links to tips, FAQs, and Web sites round out the site.

The Macintosh extensions guide

http://www.madison-web.com/ext/
Although this site has not been supported or updated since 1997, it still contains a great many descriptions of hundreds of Mac extensions, control panels, and enablers.

Want to find something Macintosh

http://w3.trib.com/~dwood/mac.html
This site is a collection of links to other more-specific Mac issues like tech help, software, games, magazines, and older Macs. There is a great set of links to sites that deal with buying and selling used Mac components.

Version Tracker online

http://www.versiontracker.com/
Many conflicts with your Mac are caused by not having the proper updated software. This site lists the latest

versions of software to use on your Mac. The updates are linked so you can download them immediately. A special Update Highlights section informs you of recent important updates you should have. Finally, there is a search engine that lets you keyword search for updates and sort them. Updates are noted if they are beta, shareware, freeware, or commercial. If you are new to the Mac community, investigate their top picks.

News Sites

There are several Macintosh Web sites that provide daily news about the Mac platform. These are great places to learn about system software conflicts, hardware problems, fixes, and just about everything Mac.

AppleLinks

http://www.AppleLinks.com
Reviews and regular features like the Farr Site and Business Mac Forum, daily Mac and technology news, software upgrades as well as software by category or title are featured here. A forum area lets you discuss topics of the day. Several online mailing lists can be delivered to your e-mail box with a free subscription. Their search engine queries companies so you can get the best possible prices.

MacCentral

http://www.maccentral.com/
Daily News stories written and published as they happen along with columns, features, and special reports are featured. Message and tip forums allow you to post and read. An electronic newsletter, *MacCentral Direct*, is a daily newsletter with content indexed in HTML format. MacCentral also publishes *iMac Daily* and *iMac Central*.

MacCentric

http://www.maccentric.com/index.shtml
MacCentric provides news about the Mac, but also has areas for the old Apple Newton, user groups, some shareware, search engines, and other links.

MaCNN—The Macintosh news network

http://www.macnn.com/
Daily news, software reviews, and opinions make this site a must visit. There are a great list of links to Mac resources and a searchable database of previous news and software.

MacinStart.com/

http://www.MacinStart.com/
Formerly MacMania, this site has news, features, game info, features, many links, and a Web directory.

Macnews.net

http://macnews.net/
Updated every 24 hours, MacNews provides about 25 stories a day. An archive lets you search previous news and there is a keyword search engine available. MacNews is available in English, Spanish, German, French, and Italian.

Macresource page

http://www.macresource.com/
This is a no-nonsense daily news page relating to Mac subjects. RAMWatch (find the best prices) and MacOSWatch (software updates) are part of this site. The site has a search engine that gives you access to the last three years' worth of news. You can also download selected software and the site has an organized section of links to other Mac sites.

MacTimes network

http://www.mactimes.com/

There is lots of current up to the minute news on this site. There are also features, editorials, links to other MacWeb sites, financial information, recent software updates that you can download, top stories, software and hardware reviews, and even a section for older Macs.

The MacHound channel grabs other interesting Mac-related stories from around the Web and other Mac sites. This site may not be in existence by the time you read this, as it was for sale.

Using the Web Search Engines to Find Help

Net search engines

You can find a great deal of information relating to fixing and upgrading your Mac on the Net as we saw above. However, there is new information being added to the Net each day; how do you keep up with this avalanche of material? Use an Internet search engine.

An Internet search engine is like your local library collection but much bigger. It is more extensive as the virtual bookshelves are global, and are by far more up to date. Some search engines update their databanks every hour. No library could afford to purchase that many books.

There are many search engines available, and while they all index information on the Net, not all do it equally.

Search engines work on two principles. First, if you want to find all information on a particular subject and access it regardless of where it is geographically, there are many search engines available to you and several of the best ones will be described later.

Most Net search engines allow you to perform detailed searches using various techniques. You can search combinations of words on what is known as Boolean logic, using connector words like AND or OR. Or, you can search by typing in words, or phrases separated by commas. You can even search on a specific phrase by enclosing it in quotes.

Not all search engines process their information the same way, so you need to try them all and see which one gives you the best results. There are search engines that actually search several other search engines at the same time for you. These are known as a *metasearch engine* and several will be described below.

Today's Net search engines also offer you the latest news, shopping, travel information, free e-mail accounts, and other information. Some let you customize their home page so you tailor the information presented each time you log on to their site. More important, they all give you the tools to search the Net as well as Usenet, and other online databases for some.

Using Sherlock

Until the introduction of Apple's System 8.5, the only way to search the Net was to visit a search engine, or a Web site which listed several search engines. Apple's new search tool Sherlock, has made searching the Net a breeze.

Sherlock works on the principle of plug-ins. If a Web site has a Sherlock Plug-in, you drop the plug-in in your "Internet Search Sites" folder located in the System Folder. When you launch Sherlock (**Command-F**), you have the option of searching on all sites, or any combination of sites that are in the menu. Sherlock initially came with a set of plug-ins for the major search engines but there are many new Sherlock plug-ins. The Web site Apple Donuts (**http://www.apple-donuts.com/sherlocksearch/ index.html**) lists more than 300 Sherlock plug-ins that cover the fields of commerce, companies, computers, entertainment (movies, television, magazines, etc.), financial, gaming, government, health, information (dictionaries, reference material), Internet/search sites, Macintosh only, mailing lists, news sites, recipes, schools, software, special Interest/other, and travel sites.

Be sure to give Sherlock plenty of memory if you plan on using lots of plug-ins.

Top net search engines

Use your Web browser to use any of these great search sites.

Alta Vista
http://www.altavista.com/
Alta Vista lets you search special categories like computers, software, and hardware. It also has search engines for Usenet and finding people, travel, entertainment products, and other consumer oriented sites, ABC news summaries, and other highlights. It offers you a free e-mail account.

When you conduct a search on Alta Vista, this search engine gives you 10 hits at a time. Each hit has a title linked to the site, a one-sentence summary or description, URL, date last modified, page size, and the ability to translate the page into another language. This last feature is a great tool.

Excite
http://www.excite.com/
Excite displays searchable topics arranged in predefined categories, as well as top news stories. It is a great search tool and lets you personalize the home page to your liking. Type in a keyword or phrase and you get more than just a list of hits. You are given a choice of additional search terms, suggested Web sites on your topic, news articles, and suggested Usenet newsgroups.

You get 10 hits at a time. Each gives the title as a live link, a summary, and the URL for the site. An added feature attached to each hit is the ability is to search for more matching sites. If one of the hits looks like something you want, the search engine will go and try to find more just like it.

Galaxy
http://www.einet.net/index.html
Galaxy is a search engine that lets you search by keyword or phrase and advanced search techniques. Its home page is a directory of categories that include business and commerce, community, engineering and technology, government, humanities, law, leisure and recreation, medicine, reference, science and social science.

Subcategories follow supercategories. When you select a category's subcategory, it presents you with a choice of articles to read, collections to view, directory listings, non-profit organizations , periodicals, and other categories if appropriate. You can type in your own keyword if none of the selection suits you.

Google
http://www.google.com/
One of the newest and most accurate search engines. Google conducts a complicated mathematical analysis of over a billion hyperlinks on the Web, and then returns the results.

HotBot
http://www.hotbot.com/
HotBot gives you several search options from the start such as the ability to search on any part or parts of words or phrases in several languages, Boolean terms, the title of a Web page, or even a link. You also have the option to search based on time, from unlimited to the last two years. You can order up the hits to be present in groups of 10 to 100 and decide if you want full descriptions, summaries, or just the URLs. You can

insist that pages include either images, audio, video, or JavaScript.

A section on technology lets you read reviews of software and hardware, download software, and get tools for working on your Web page. There is a link to HotWired, the online version of *Wired* magazine.

With HotBot you can also search Usenet, the yellow and white pages, look for e-mail addresses or domain names, jobs and resumés, classifieds, homes and loans, stocks, downloads, music, and even get road maps.

Infoseek
www.infoseek.com
Infoseek presents categories and subcategories for quick searching; or use a keyword or phrase search engine. Four search categories are present: Web sites, news, companies (business), and Usenet newsgroups.

Search results give you a listing of directory topics that are also searchable, with a group of 10 hits that give a clickable title, summary date, size, and URL. You can also find similar pages and grouped results. Suppose a Web site has a number of related links on the site. Instead of trying to find each one, Infoseek presents them all to you on a page, one Web site at a time.

Lycos
http://www.lycos.com/
Lycos is organized into Web guides. Select a category to see links to resources pertaining in that category. You can search by keyword or phrases.

Magellan
http://www.mckinley.com/
Magellan is similar to Lycos: it is arranged as Web guides, categories of frequently sought after information. You can keyword or phrase search the entire Web or Green Light sites only. Green Light sites are ones

which have been reviewed and contained no adult-only content at the time of review, so are child safe.

Your search results are returned by relevance (more relevant at the top), and presented 10 at a time. Both the title and URL are clickable, a summary is included. You have the option to find similar pages from any hit.

Snap
http://home.snap.com/
Snap has searchable categories on its home page similar to those of other search engines. In the computing area there is a dedicated Mac section. Each section on Snap also provides a top ten, or best of, set of links that pertain to the category.

Starting Point
http://www.stpt.com/
Starting Point lets you search by keyword on any topic. You also have the choice to search other engines, yellow pages, and other guides. Categories are arranged into channels which you can select, or you can select each category and do a keyword search. A great feature is the ability to view new submissions in all categories in real time.

WebCrawler
www.webcrawler.com
Webcrawler organizes its home page into channels. You can search by keyword or phrase on the whole database or each channel, but unlike the other search engines, the resulting list of 25 hits only gives you the title of the site which is linked. This is good if you know exactly what you are searching for.

You do have the option to obtain summaries of the hits though, which gives you the title, summary, and URL, and the option to search for similar pages. A shortcuts section lists news groups based on your topics and also gives you options for checking Web sites that you might be interested in.

Yahoo
www.yahoo.com
Yahoo's home page provides several organized subject categories ready for exploring. You can search by keyword or phrase and there are several advanced search techniques available.

Yahoo gives you a listing of categories that have your keyword highlighted when you search for a topic, instead of getting a list of 10 or more hits. By selecting a category, you are then brought to another page that will have a listing of sites with title and summary. The title is clickable. You have the option to search more of Yahoo or just the category you are in.

Metasearch engines

Metasearch engines are Web sites that search more than one search engine at a time. The advantage of using a metasearch engine is saving time, since you are only using one engine to search several.

All In One
http://www.albany.net/allinone/all1www.html
There are over 400 links to search engines and other data collections on one page. Just find the one you want to search, type in your keywords, and hit the return key.

Cyber411
http://www.cyber411.com/
Cyber411 checks 16 other search engines at the same time for your keywords. It has advanced search functions also.

Mamma
http://www.mamma.com/
Mamma searches the Web, Usenet, news, stocks, and other categories. Options on searching are available. It contains other databases like reverse lookup, telephone directories, map making, etc.

Savvy Search
www.savvysearch.com
Savvy Search checks over 150 search engines, guides, auctions, storefronts, Usenet archives, news archives, shareware libraries at once.

The Ultimate Internet Search Index
http://www.geocities.com/SiliconValley/Heights/ 5296/index.html
This site has several categories of search engines available to you from the mainstream engines, to e-mail address lookup, shopping, newsgroups, mailing lists, software files, and much more.

Better to Be Safe Than Sorry

As the old proverb goes, an ounce of prevention is worth a pound of cure. However, there are times when bad luck hits even those who take every precaution. There will be a time when you start up your Mac and nothing happens. No hard drive appears on the desktop, the disk won't read when you insert it in the floppy drive, or the screen is blank. Time for Dr. Mac.

Fortunately, there are many great programmers in the Mac community who have created various disk and software recovery programs that can help you recover lost files, floppies, removable media, and hard drives. Some of these programs check the condition of your hardware, looking for bad blocks on a hard drive, or making sure your RAM is working right. There are other programs that will get into your hard drive and bring it back to the desktop, or fix a specific file that is damaged, or automatically scan the disk while you are working to look for potential problems and alert you before these happen. It's a good investment to own one or two of these programs.

A good disk recovery program is like having a fire extinguisher near by, or a first aid kit in the glove compartment. Most times you don't need it but when you do, it's a life saver. This chapter will introduce you to a few of them.

Four Life Savers

Apple's Disk First Aid

Apple's Disk First Aid is a free diagnostic repair program that comes with the Mac and is usually located in the utilities folder. Disk First Aid will check for and attempt to correct damage to the directories and catalog files on your hard drive or floppies, but it does not check individual files for corruption.

It is set up to scan your hard drive after a crash when you restart (Figure 6.1). It verifies the directory structure of any Mac disk or volume (both standard HFS or OS Extended [HFS Plus from version 8.1 or later]).

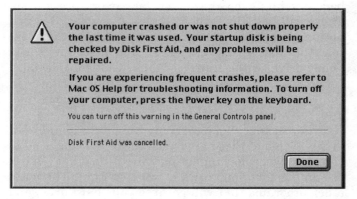

Figure 6.1 Disk First Aid automatically starts after a computer crash.

You cannot repair the startup disk with Disk First Aid. You have to initiate repair from another hard drive, or floppy. Disk Aid cannot repair the disk or floppy it is residing on, or any disk that has File Sharing enabled.

Apple suggests that you bring up Disk First Aid's status screen before you run the test. Then, after you open the drive, type **Command-S**, then check the drive. You'll see a comprehensive list of actions performed.

Disk First Aid is useful if you use another disk recovery program and it is not compatible with Apple's extended format and causes a problem. Disk First Aid will attempt to correct that problem.

Using Disk First Aid is fairly simple. Select the volume or disk and select **Verify**. If you find a problem then you select the **Repair** button (Figure 6.2).

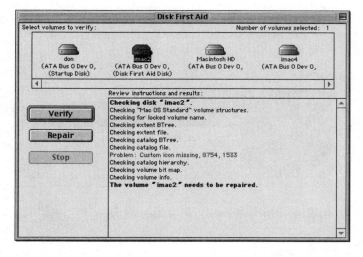

Figure 6.2 After selecting a volume to scan, Disk First Aid reports its activities to you.

Obviously, you do not have the kind of control over repairs as you do with TechTool or other disk recovery programs, but Disk First Aid is a good first step.

TechTool Pro 2.5

TechTool by MicroMat Computer Systems (**www. micromat.com**) has been around for some time.

TechTool Pro 2.5 is compatible with FireWire drives, USB removable drives (like those from Imation and Newer Technology), the latest G3 and G4 Macs, and is fully compatible with System 9.0.

TechTool Pro main application

TechTool is a multifaceted program and comes as a bootable CD so it will work with all flavors of the Mac. Use this part of the program to run a variety of low-level diagnostic and repair tests. You have a choice of three interfaces to run these tests: Simple (Figure 6.3), Standard (Figure 6.4), and Expert (Figure 6.5). This allows you to let the program run everything for you; or you can select an individual test in expert mode.

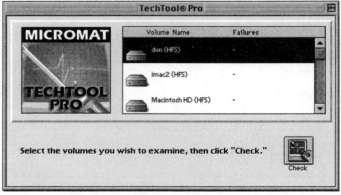

Figure 6.3   MicroMat's Tech Tool Simple Interface is the easiest to use.

This suite of programs actually checks your hardware and software for problems and corrects them (or asks you to) (Figure 6.6). After it runs a battery of tests it gives you a complete report on what it found, repaired, and other advice which you can print out (Figure 6.7).

It also allows you to rebuild a volume, optimize the disk, recover files, and perform individual tests on everything from audio to the condition of your video

RAM. If you are suspicious of a specific condition about your Mac you can run that individual test. For example, you can select each individual key on your keyboard and test it.

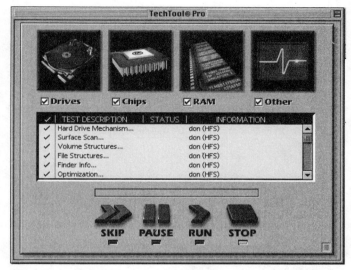

Figure 6.4 TechTool's Standard Interface lets you decide which tests to perform.

Figure 6.5 TechTool's Expert Interface gives you more control on which tests to run.

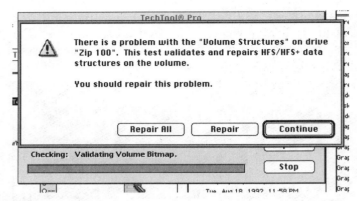

Figure 6.6 TechTool gives you the option to repair a problem when it is found.

Figure 6.7 After completion, TechTool gives you a complete report of its findings.

Protection control panel

Besides the main application program this control panel allows you to periodically save "protection" files, invisible backup files of critical drive catalog data. Protection files allow the TechTool Pro application to easily recover lost files or volumes (Figure 6.8).

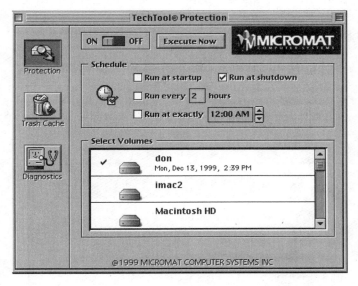

Figure 6.8 The Protection Panel allows you to recover lost files and volumes when set.

This tool provides an important "undelete" mechanism so that if you trash a file accidentally, empty the trash, then realize later you want the file back, you can open the Protection Control panel and recover the lost file by dragging it to the desktop.

Trash Cache saves all deleted files, so it's a great tool for recovering any kind of file. According to the makers of TechTool, many software programs create invisible "scratch" files. The program will continually create and delete these files as you work. Even if you forget to use the Save command and then your Mac crashes, you can possibly save most of your work by recovering the scratch file.

Also with this control panel you can add automation for a quick check of your drive at intervals you set.

TechTool allows you to perform preventive measures like easily rebuilding the desktop (and saving the Get Info box data) and zapping PRAM. It retails for around $90.

Norton Utilities 5.0

Norton Utilities, published by Symantec Corporation, has for years dominated the Mac recovery arena. It is a suite of six applications designed to keep your Mac in good running order (Figure 6.9).

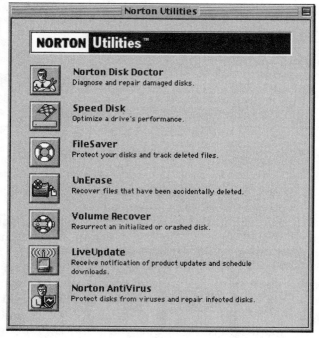

Figure 6.9   Norton Utilities gives you a set of disk recovery options.

Disk Doctor diagnoses and then repairs damaged disks (Figure 6.10).

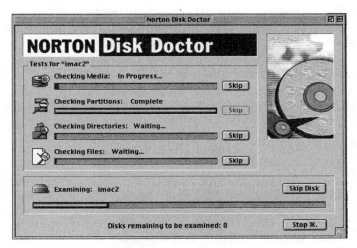

Figure 6.10 Disk Doctor shows you progress bars while it is working and gives you the option to repair any problems.

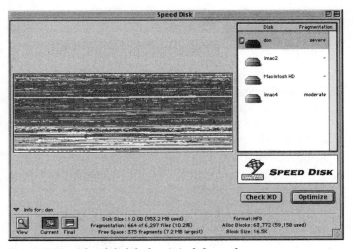

Figure 6.11 A hard disk before it is defragged.

Speed Disk is an optimization program that will put files back together in one place and speed up the performance of accessing information (Figure 6.11). Speed Disk is unlike other disk optimizers, which do not optimize files that are larger than the amount of free disk space. Speed Disk can optimize a disk different ways for different applications, from CD recording to multimedia (Figure 6.12).

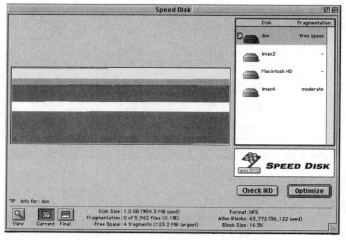

Figure 6.12   The same hard disk after running Speed Disk.

FileSaver allows you to choose which disks to scan, protect, and track. It scans your drive for problems at shutdown and saves your disk's directory structure to help recover lost files in case of problems (Figure 6.13).

Unerase allows you to retrieve files you already threw into the trash and deleted (Figure 6.14).

Volume Recover lets you scan a damaged disk and recover files (Figure 6.15).

LiveUpdate takes you to Symantec's Web site to download the latest updates to the program (Figure 7.16).

Finally, if you have Norton's AntiVirus application installed it will show up in the main Norton panel, giving you easy access to anti-virus checking (Figure 6.17).

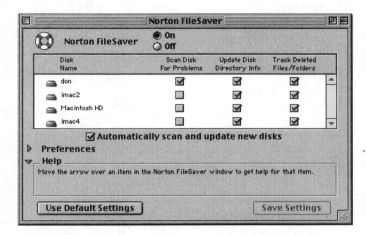

Figure 6.13 Filesaver will save your disk's directory structure when you shutdown.

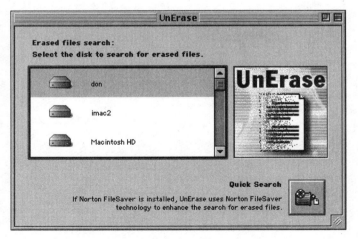

Figure 6.14 UnErase will recover files you accidently tossed in the trash can and deleted.

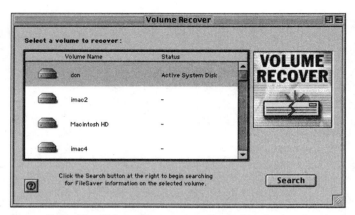

Figure 6.15   Use Volume Recover to salvage files from a damaged disk.

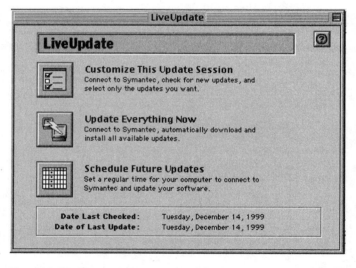

Figure 6.16   Be sure you are using the latest version of Norton Utilities with LiveUpdate, a tool that automatically goes onto the Net and downloads the most recent version.

The main new feature of Norton Utilities 5.0 is the introduction to Norton Disk Doctor of Live Repair. Previous versions made you use the bootable CD to repair a problem. Now you can repair the startup volume directly, no matter where Disk Doctor is residing.

Norton retails for around $45 and AntiVirus costs about $25. For less than $100 you have a very reliable set of recovery applications.

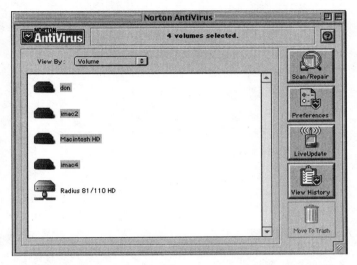

Figure 6.17 You can keep virus free by using Norton's AntiVirus regularly.

Data Rescue 2.1.1

Data Rescue is a tool by Sylvain Demongeot that is specifically designed for recovering lost Macintosh volumes (Figure 6.18).

It recovers files and folders from crashed hard disks, floppy disks, or removable cartridges (Zip, Jazz, magneto-optical, etc.). Your recovered data are saved to another medium, such as a Zip or floppy, leaving the original disk untouched. Since it is a small program, only 300KB, it fits neatly on a floppy.

Data Rescue operates a little differently from Norton Utilities and other data recovery programs that search and recover file fragments. Data Rescue searches for catalog fragments instead, and then recovers them, including restoring icons, dates, and even folder hierarchy if needed. The catalog file keeps track of other files and folders and contains valuable information about files such as their size, type, hierarchy, and where they are located on the disk.

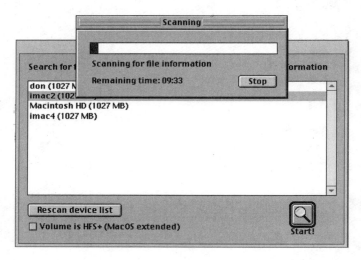

Figure 6.18   Data Rescue is a crash recovery tool and retrieves files from damaged disks.

Data Rescue does not work if you have already thrown a file in the trash by mistake, since it is no longer listed in the catalog. If you have reinitialized a volume by mistake, the catalog is completely erased, so Data Rescue can't help you there either.

Data Rescue is perfect for salvaging a crashed floppy. It recovers HFS+ (MacOS Extended) volumes and works with System 8.5.

Data Rescue is shareware and costs $39. You can download a demo of the program at the Wild Bits home page (**http://www.wildbits.com/rescue/**) that lets you recover one file per session.

There's More!

While Disk First Aid, TechTool, Norton Utilities, and Data Rescue are superb programs they are not the only ones that can help in a jam. Other useful programs that have had good reviews are described below.

Auto-Save 1.01

If you are using an application that does not automatically save your work or have adjustable settings, Auto-Save from Buzz Mac Software may be useful to you. It allows you to create an automatic save preference based on whatever time interval you set for each application you use. Select which applications you would like Auto-Save to work on. Select what script you would like to use to perform the save. Then set the time intervals in which you would like the auto save to occur. It's that simple (Figure 6.19).

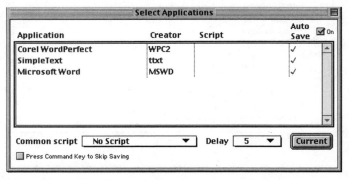

Figure 6.19 AutoSave does just that, saves your work at regular intervals that you set.

Auto save is shareware for $15. You can download the program at **http://www.buzzmac.com**.

Spring Cleaning

Spring Cleaning by Aladdin Systems (**www. aladdinsys.com**) is an innovative house cleaning product for the Mac. It searches through 12 routines on your hard drive to see what files and applications you don't want or need (Figure 6.20).

Figure 6.20 Spring Cleaning helps you manage all the files in your system folder.

It checks for structurally invalid files, invisible files, duplicate fonts or files, old aliases, and more. It is quite easy to bloat up your system with unwanted preference files and files you don't need or use anymore (Figure 6.21). Spring Cleaning retails for around $25.

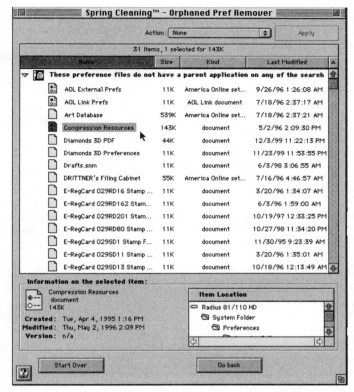

Figure 6.21   You can delete a whole range of unwanted files with Spring Cleaning.

CanOpener 4.0

CanOpener by Abbott Systems is probably one of the most important pieces of software you can own. This is a must-have software utility you will develop genuine affection for. This program gives you emergency access to any Mac file, especially damaged ones.

If you end up with a corrupted data file you can easily extract the text or images with CanOpener so you can recover almost anything that gets damaged. You can even view virus infected files, recover the information, and not launch the virus.

CanOpener reads the formats of over 25 image files and lets you convert pictures between different formats. It has special filters to extract names, phone numbers, URLs, e-mail, Web and IP address, strip HTML coding, remove extra carriage returns and blank spaces from e-mail and Web text, extract sentences such as questions or anything containing $'s and numbers, and rapidly find clean text in files that contain huge amounts of "garbage."

It's priced at $65 and you can get it directly from Abbott Systems (**http://www.abbottsystems.com/**) (Figure 6.22).

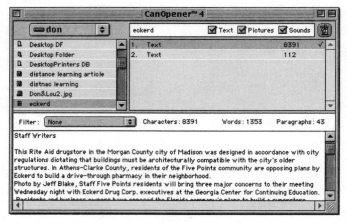

Figure 6.22   CanOpener will go into any damaged file and retrieve text or images.

Clean-Install Assistant 1.2

This little program can save you time after you recover from a crash and need to reinstall your system software. One of the major headaches in doing a clean install of system software is that you lose all your preferences, special files and settings that you created in the old system. In order to continue using them you must go back in the old system folder and drag out those important files and place them in your new clean system folder.

First, you have to remember which files you need to transfer and that can be a real pain. Clean Install does all the work for you. It scans your system folder before you do a clean install and gathers up all those special files and places them on hold. After you do your clean install it then places all those files into the new clean system folder for you.

Clean Install Assistant is free for personal use and businesses with three or fewer Macs. Other users may purchase a license. Download it from author Marc Moini's Web site (**http://www.marcmoini.com**). It is System 9 compatible (Figure 6.23).

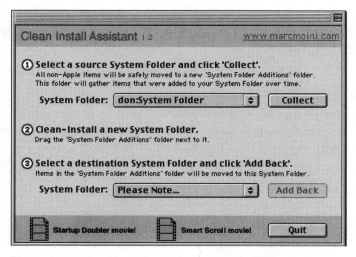

Figure 6.23 Use Clean Install before you install a new system folder to avoid loosing any important files in the existing system folder.

7

G3 Upgrade Paths for G3 and Non-G3 Macs

Upgrading your G3 is a snap, thanks to Apple's ZIF (Zero Insertion Force) technology. With the G3 computers, it's a matter of taking out the existing processor and snapping in a new one. Moreover, several third-party developers have designed an upgrade path for those non-G3 Macintosh computers you may still own, even the Mac clones.

Upgrading an older PowerMac to a G3 processor is as simple as adding a Nubus or PCI card, or a daughter card. You can use a ZIF Adapter, or carrier card, which allows a ZIF module to work. In older PowerMacs you insert a daughter card into the PDS ("processor direct slot").

Processor upgrades vary in price depending on company, speed, which model of Mac you are using the processor on, and other features like the amount of cache. Prices range from several hundred dollars to over $1,000.

Several companies offer G3 upgrades covering almost every PowerMac from the 6100 up. Prices vary, however, and some models get retired as faster upgrades take their place. A few models have been discontinued, especially those that worked on some of the Mac clones. However, you can often find used models on Mac Web sites, or from those companies that specialize in offering "pre-owned" equipment.

You can purchase upgrades from the companies direct, although PowerLogix has discontinued selling directly to end-users. Mac mail-order companies often offer products from several different vendors so you can compare price and performance.

There are now G4 upgrades on the market. However, as of this writing there were not enough to list. Check the various Web sites listed below. Unfortunately, the iMac and iBook are not upgradable at the present time.

Buying by Mail Order or from Online Web Merchants

The obvious advantage of ordering upgrades from mail-order companies is that you often save 20% or more on products, do not pay for sales tax and often do not pay for shipping. The better mail-order companies also stand behind the product and will work hard to keep you a satisfied customer.

There are many mail-order companies that offer Mac products but only a few that really specialize in the Mac line. Most have similar in pricing on both hardware and software; often the difference is only pennies. They have good delivery and return policies. Each has a Web site so you can order online, and most are open 24 hours for phone orders. I prefer talking to a representative before I place an order.

Most of these companies sell both PC and Mac products; the difference is staffing and a different phone number, but they are usually located in the same building: MacConnection has a PCConnection. MacWarehouse has a PCWarehouse. MacMall is also PCMall, and so on. If you need to discuss PC compatibility, simply ask for that toll free number or to be transferred.

Before you order a product, be sure to ask if it is in stock. Unscrupulous mail order companies will charge your credit card even if they do not have the item in stock. You could wait several weeks before you get the product, but they have your money.

Web merchant sites tailored to the Mac platform are often run by Mac fanatics and are a good source of information and bargain prices. Unfortunately, some have turned to the online auction craze (thanks to Ebay and the like), which I think is a waste of time.

MacConnection

http://www.macconnection.com/
MacConnection is one of the oldest Mac mail-order companies (15 years). If you belong to a Mac User Group, you get free ground shipping on your order. The company has good prices and support. The toll-free number is 1-800 MAC LISA. You can ask for a hard-copy catalog or visit their Web site.

MacMall

http://www.cc-inc.com/home.asp
MacMall is another mail-order company that produces a hard copy catalog but you can order from their Web site as well. The toll free number is (800) 222-2808.

ClubMac

http://www.clubmac.com/
ClubMac offers a hard-copy catalog and a Web site. Call them toll free at (800) 258-2622.

MacWarehouse

http://www.warehouse.com/macwarehouse
MacWarehouse's catalog averages 100 pages, and once you are on their mailing list you will get them often.

You can call (800) 622-6222 and request a copy or visit the Web site.

Absolute Mac

http://www.absolutemac.com/

This is an excellent site to buy Macs and peripherals. One great feature lets you write the specs of what you want to buy, to over 30 resellers. If you check the section on upgrade cards, there is a listing of prices offered by several mail-order or online merchants. This is a good place to start comparative shopping.

Memory

Adding memory to your G3 computers is easy but the cost of memory varies considerably. Check around for the best prices. RAM costs have been rising. Listed in the table below are Apple's recommended maximum RAM sizes. However, third-party manufacturers have been able to make larger capacity RAM modules so be sure to check the latest news on the Web sites of RAMWatch or Chip Merchant.

Chip Merchant

http://www.chipmerchant.com/

Chip Merchant is the best place to buy memory modules for your G3 Mac. I have always found them to have the best prices overall and they stand behind their product for life. Keep your receipt. I once returned a memory module that went bad and it was over 3 years old.

RAMWatch

http://www.macresource.pair.com/mrp/ramwatch.shtml

This is a great place to check before you buy RAM. RAMWatch keeps track of several companies and offers the lowest and average prices. I still personally recommend Chip Merchant for best overall prices and support, but it does not hurt to investigate this site first.

Memory Upgrade Path

Model	Standard memory	Maximum memory	No. of slots
Apple iMac (233-266-333 MHz models)	32MB (Removable)	256MB	2 (SO-DIMM SDRAM) In order to upgrade to 256MB you must insert 127MB in top and a shorter 128MB in the bottom slot
Apple iMac (350 MHz models)	64MB (Removable)	512MB	2 (two PC100 SDRAM)
Apple iMac DV (400 MHz models)	64MB (Removable)	512MB	2 (two PC100 SDRAM)
Apple iMac DV SE (400 MHz models)	128MB (Removable)	512MB	2 (two PC100 SDRAM)
Apple Macintosh Server G3 M6389LL/A	64MB (Removable)	384MB	3
Apple Macintosh Server G3 M6461LL/A	128MB (Removable)	384MB	3
Apple Power Macintosh G3 (Desktop)	32MB (Removable)	192MB	3
Apple Power Macintosh G3 (Tower)	32MB (Removable)	384MB	3
Apple Power Macintosh G3 All-in-one	32MB (Removable)	384MB	384MB

(Continued)

Model	Standard memory	Maximum memory	No. of slots
Apple Power Macintosh G3 (B&W)	64 MB or 128 MB (Removable)	1 GB	4
Notes: PC100 SDRAM DIMMs			
Apple PowerBook G3 (grey case)	32 MB (Nonremovable)	160 MB	1
Apple PowerBook G3 (black case)	32MB or 64MB (Removable)	384 MB	2
PowerBook G3 Series (Bronze keyboard)	64 MB	384 MB	2
iBook	32 MB (Nonremovable)	160 MB	1

Processor/Accelerator Upgrade Path

Several companies such as Newer Technology, Sonnet Technologies, Vimage Corporation, and others offer a variety of G3 upgrade products that can bring even the earliest PowerMacs and compatibles up to G3 speed and performance. The following tables list the most recent products available, but be sure to visit their Web sites for new additions and the best prices.

For Desktops and Minitowers

Manufacturer	Speed	Cache size and speed	Made for
Newer Technology http://www.newertech.com/			
MAXpowr G3			
300/200	300MHz	1MB at 200MHz	Power Macintosh
400/200	400MHz	1MB at 200MHz	7500/100
500/250	500MHz	1MB at 250MHz	7600/120
			7600/132
			8500/120
			8500/132
			8500/150

(Continued)

Manufacturer	Speed	Cache size and speed	Made for
			8515/120
			9500/120
			9500/132
			9500/150
			9515/132
			7300/166
			7300/180
			7300/180–PC Compatible
			7300/200
			7600/200
			8500/180
			8600/200
			8600/250
			8600/300
			9500/200
			9600/200
			9600/200
			9600/233
			9600/300
			9600/350
			9500/180MP
			9600/200MP
			UMAX J700
			UMAX S900
			Power Computing Power Curve, Power Center, Power Center Pro, PowerTower, PowerTower Pro, PowerWave

Manufacturer	Video support	Speed	Cache size and speed	Made for
Newer Technology http://www.newertech.com/ MAXpowr G3 PDS				
PowerMac 6100	Yes	up to 266MHz	512k at 2:1 ratio	Power Mac 6100/60
PowerMac 7100/8100	Yes	up to 300MHz	512k at 3:2 ratio	6100/60AV 6100/66

(Continued)

Manufacturer	Video support	Speed	Cache size and speed	Made for
				6100/66AV
				6100/66 DOS Compatible
				Performa 6110
				Performa 6112
				Performa 6115
				Performa 6116
				Performa 6117
				Performa 6118
				7100/66
				7100/66AV
				7100/80
				7100/80AV
				8100/80
				8100/80AV
				8100/100
				8100/100AV
				8100/110
				8100/110AV
				8115/110AV

Manufacturer	Speed	Cache size and speed	Made for Power Mac G3
Newer Technology http://www.newertech.com/			
MAXpowr G3-G3			
400/200	400MHz	1MB at 200MHz	(Beige)
500/250	500MHz	1MB at 250MHz	(Blue and White)
MAXpowr G3-L2			
300/150	300MHz	512k at 150MHz	Power Macintosh
300/200	300MHz	1MB at 200MHz	4400
			4400 DOS
			7220 (International)
			5400
			5500
			6400
			6500
			Performa 5400
			Performa 5410
			Performa 5420
			Performa 5430

(Continued)

Manufacturer	Speed	Cache size and speed	Made for
			Performa 5440
			Performa 6360
			Performa 6400
			Performa 6410
			Performa 6420
			UMAX C-500
			UMAX C-600
			Motorola
			StarMax 3000
			StarMax 4000
			StarMax 5000
			StarMax 5500
			Power- Computing PowerBase (all)
			APS M*Power Series (all)

MAXpowr Carrier Card *(discontinued–look for used ones)*

MAXpowr G3-CC	n/a	n/a	Power Mac 7300
			7500
MAXpowr G3-CC 400	400MHz	200MHz	7600
			8500
MAXpowr G3-CC 500	500MHz	250MHz	8600
			9500
			9600
			PowerComputing
			PowerTower,
			PowerTower Pro,
			PowerCenter,
			PowerCenter Pro,
			PowerWave,
			PowerCurve
			UMAX J700
			UMAXS900 series
			Daystar Genesis MP series

Manufacturer	Speed	L2 cache size and speed	Made for
Sonnet Technologies http://www.sonnettech.com			
Crescendo G3/NuBus			
250/512	240–266 MHz	125 MHz/512K	Performa 6110, 6112, 6115, 6116,
266/1M	240–266 MHz	125 MHz/1M	6117, 6118 Power Mac
300/512	300 MHz	150 MHz/512K	Workgroup
300/1M	300 MHz	150 MHz/1M	Server 6150,
400/1M	400 MHz	200 MHz/1M	8150, 9150 PowerComputing 100, 120 Radius System 100, 81/110
Crescendo G3/PCI			
266/512, 300/512, 300/1M, 400/1M, 466/1M, 500/1M			Power Mac 7300 Power Mac 7500 Power Mac 7600 Power Mac 8500 Power Mac 8515 Power Mac 8600 Power Mac 9500 Power Mac 9515 Power Mac 9600 Power Mac Workgroup Server 7350, 8550, 9650 Power-Computing PowerTower Pro, PowerWave UMAX J700 UMAX S900 DayStar Genesis Series, Millennium Mactell XB Pro
Encore G3			
466/1M			G3 Desktop
500/1M			Mini Tower Server All-In-One

(Continued)

Manufacturer	Speed	L2 cache size and speed	Made for
			G3 Blue and White

Manufacturer	Speed	Backside cache	Made for
Vimage Corporation http://www.vimagestore.com/index.html			
PF G3/240			
PF G3/240	240	512KB	Performa and Power Macintosh 6360, 54xx, 55xx, 64xx, 65xx
Vpower PM4400			
G3/240	240	512KB	Apple Power Mac 4400
G3//300	300	1MB	Motorola Star Max 3000, 4000
Vpower G3			
Vpower G3	233	512KB	Apple Power Macintosh 7300/166, 7300/180, 7500/100, 7600/120, 7600/132, 7600/200, 8500/120, 8500/132, 8500/150, 8500/180, 8600/200ZIP, 8600/250, 9500/120, 9500/132, 9500/150, 9500/180MP, 9500/200, 9600/200MP, 9600/233, 9600/300, 9600/350
Vpower G3	300	1MB	

(Continued)

Manufacturer	Speed	Backside cache	Made for
			UMAX Pulsar 1500, 1660, 2000, 2000VR, 2000DP 2250, 2330, 2330VR, 2500, 2500DP

Manufacturer	Speed	Backside cache	Made for
PowerLogix http://www.powerlogix.com			
PowerForce G3			
250/125/512K	250	512K	Power Macintosh
300/150/1Mb	300	1Mb	7300, 7500,
400/200/1Mb	400	1Mb	7600, 8500,
466/183/1Mb	466	1Mb	8600, 9500,
500/250/1Mb	500	1Mb	9600
ZIF 500/250/			Power-
1Mb	500	1Mb	Computing
ZForce	500		PowerBase,
(Adapts			PowerWave,
ZIF-style			PowerCurve,
processor			PowerCenter,
modules for			PowerCenter
use in			Pro, PowerTower,
PCI-based			PowerTower Pro;
PowerMacs)			UMAX/SuperMac
			S900, J700
			DayStar
			Millenium and
			Genesis

For Powerbooks

Manufacturer	Speed	Backside cache	Made for
Vimage Corporation http://www.vimagestore.com/index.html			
Vpower PB1400 G3			
G3 233	233	512KB	1400cs/117
G3 266	266		1400c/117
			1400cs/133
			1400c/133
			1400cs/166
			1400c/166

Manufacturer	Speed	Backside cache size and bus speed	Made for
Newer Technology http://www.newertech.com/			
NUpowr 1400			
NUpowr 216MHz/512K/ 108MHz	216MHz	512K/108MHz	PowerBook 1400
NUpowr 250MHz/1MB/ 125MHz	250MHz	1MB/125MHz	
Nupowr G3 2400			
Nupowr G3 2400 240/160	240MHz	1MB	PowerBook 2400

Buying Used Parts

You can get bargain prices by searching Web sites that offer used Mac products for sale. Most of the good sites offer a bulletin board or chat area where you can discuss or rate buyers or sellers. Be warned that there are people who will sell defective merchandise. You need to do your homework and not send cash to anyone. The best payment method is COD. You get the product then pay for it. It's easy to track your purchase as well.

Boston Computer Exchange

http://www.bocoex.com/

Boston Computer Exchange is one of the oldest wholesale and retail dealers in new, used, and refurbished PCs, and was founded in 1982. There is an auction site where businesses can bid on items, new and used computers, and peripherals. Inventory is hit and miss on Mac products.

Class Mac

http://www.classmac.com/

This site allows you to place and read ads. A Feedback Forum lets you offer praise, recommendations, complaints, ideas, and suggestions. Class Mac is now part of the online auction craze with AuctionMac.com where you can bid on Mac items. You can search their database for items in their Ad section. This is a very good site.

Deal iMac

http://www.deal-mac.com/
Deal Mac (and iMac) looks for special deals on Mac hardware, peripherals, and software and gives you the list with links to those deals when possible. This is a great site to visit when you want to add to your G3 but find out first what prices are available.

Macintosh User Market (MUM)

http://www.maconcall.com/mum/index.html
In pre-Internet days the **comp.sys.mac.wanted** and the **misc.forsale** newsgroups on Usenet were the place to check for buying new and used Macs. This site was designed to fill the vacuum on the net. Both new and used Macintosh products are offered from Mac resellers, VARs, and the general public. This is basically a bulletin board. Just find the category you are looking for and read the postings.

SupportHelp.com

http://www.service911.com/
Looking for technical help from a soft- or hardware vendor? This Web site has hot links to the majority of newsgroups that provide tech support at the click of the mouse.

Index

Note:Boldface numbers indicate illustrations.

About the Author

DON RITTNER (Schenectady, NY) bought his first Mac in 1984. Soon after, he started the Mac Enthusiasts Club of the Capital Area, one of the oldest Mac user groups in the country. He has been writing about the Mac since 1985, first as a columnist and User Group Editor for *Macazine*, and later for *Mac Horizons*. Don has published more than 12 books on science, history, computers, and the Net, including *The iMac Book* (Coriolis), which was in its second printing only a few months after release.